GIANT LINERS OF THE WORLD

GIANT LINERS OF THE WORLD

ALAN L. CARY

D. APPLETON-CENTURY COMPANY
INCORPORATED
NEW YORK   LONDON
1937

PRINTED AND MADE IN GREAT BRITAIN

AUTHOR'S NOTE

IN compiling this book dealing with the sixty largest of the world's mercantile ships that have yet been built, I have been actuated by the idea of dealing with each vessel individually, so that the data of each ship is set forth under a separate heading complete with a scale silhouette and illustration.

This method enables the reader easily to find the details of each ship as required, and also makes the comparison of vessels an easy matter.

While every endeavour has been made to ensure accuracy I will welcome the pointing out of any discrepancies or important omissions.

I tender my best thanks for the valuable assistance given me by the great Shipping Companies and for the help derived from "Lloyd's" and the various shipping periodicals, also for the inspiration and help from the works of Mr. A. J. McAginnis, Mr. F. C. Bowen, Mr. Gerald Aylmer.

ALAN L. CARY.

Northfleet,
Kent.

5

CONTENTS

The tonnages given should not be taken as being perfectly accurate, as they change very frequently at each refit and re-measurement.

Building . Sister Ship to Queen Mary probable name King George V about 85,000 gr. tons.
    Holland Amerika Liner to be named Nieuw Amsterdam about 35,000 gr. tons.
    Orcades (Orient Line), about 23,500 gr. tons.
    Two Sister Ships to P. & O. Strathmore about 24,000 gr. tons to be named Stratheden and Strathallan.
    A Sister Ship to s.s. Manhattan & Washington about 24,000 gr. tons.
    A M.S. for Swedish-America Line of about 25,000 gr. tons.

MAURETANIA—
though broken by man, thy name
liveth for ever.

INTRODUCTION

FROM *BALTIC* TO *QUEEN MARY*

WITH the completion of "Britain's maritime masterpiece," the *Queen Mary*, and the placing in service of the great French Liner *Normandie* public interest in the world's ships has been aroused as, perhaps, never before, the nearest approach to this keen worldwide interest being in the year 1907 when those two historic Cunarders *Lusitania* and *Mauretania* of never to be forgotten fame took their places on the North Atlantic.

The widespread popularity of ocean cruising during the last few years has greatly added to this interest, for what person who has made a voyage in an ocean liner ever ceases to remember with affection the brave ship that was his home if even only for a week or so? Ships, even the modern steel structures with their thousands and thousands of horse-power, are living things, and every one has a personality all its own. This is just as true about our great modern liners as it was of the sailing vessels of old.

There is no pleasure in land travelling of any form that can ever equal the thrill of an ocean voyage, and the feel of a gently moving great ship under one's feet.

Since the inception of the steamship the size has steadily progressed from a few hundred tons of the early vessels, to the over eighty thousand tons of the latest triumphs of man's mastery over nature.

To the post war generation it hardly seems possible that it was only in 1902 that a steamship of what is now the modest size of 20,000 tons was constructed, it taking roughly eighty years of steamship building for this size to be reached. During the last thirty years this tonnage has been quadrupled and there is now talk by practical men of affairs of the 100,000 ton liner.

Since the year 1919 there has not only been the steady increase in size of the ocean liner but a big increase in the number of routes on which big ships are now employed. Up to the year 1920 all the world's big ships, that is those of about 20,000 tons and upwards, were exclusively on the North Atlantic and never before the Great War had a twenty thousand tonner been seen east of Suez or on the Pacific Ocean. Now these big ships are to be seen on almost all of the world's passenger routes, and the great extension of cruising has taken big ships to ports where never before had large liners been seen.

Apart from size many other changes have taken place in the world's shipping during the last two decades, one of these changes being the replacement of coal by oil as fuel by the big passenger ship, and when it is realised that

AQUITANIA

some of these powerful vessels consumed as much as 800 tons of coal each twenty-four hours, it will be readily understood how revolutionary has been the change.

Now, all large liners use oil for fuel, either for steam raising or directly in Diesel engines, and in fact in the year 1934 it was estimated that some 54 per cent of British ships were using oil fuel.

Another change has been the consolidation of its premier position, as a prime mover for the big express liner, of the Steam Turbine first introduced on the Atlantic by the Allan Liners *Victorian* and *Virginian* in the year 1905, the latter vessel being still in service as the Swedish-American Liner *Drottningholm*.

The Diesel engined Motor Ship has made its appearance among the list of big ships, this type of engine making another radical change, but up to the present no *fast* express big liner has been fitted with this form of engine, the largest being the M.S. *Augustus* of 32,650 gross tons.

Other changes on the engineering side are the adoption of the water tube boiler for marine use and the greatly increased steam pressures. The first Cunard steamers of 1840 had a steam pressure of 45 lbs. per sq. in. This had risen gradually to 180 lbs. in the *Teutonic* of 1890, after that the rise was slower until in 1914, 250 lbs. had been reached. Now 400 lbs. and super-pressure boilers of 800 lbs. per sq. in. pressure have been constructed.

The substitution of oil for coal has made many other changes, one of these being the great reduction in the number of men now carried in the engineering departments of the big express liners, as for instance when the Cunarder *Aquitania* was converted from coal to oil burning the engine-room staff was reduced by no less than three hundred men. The rapid and clean way in which the oil fuel is handled is responsible for a big increase in the earning power of the great ships as it enables these ocean monsters to be turned round in such short times that would never have been possible with coal bunkering.

Since 1928 another new form of liner drive has been adopted, the greatest example of which is the mighty *Normandie*. This new drive is the Turbo-Electric drive, which form of propulsion is, that instead of the great steam turbines driving the propellers through reduction gears and great long shafts, an electric generator is coupled direct to each turbine and the electric power is led through suitable control switch-gear to electric motors which drive the screws situated usually well aft so as to reduce the length of driving shafts. The main advantage of this form of drive is that the turbine room can be situated in the most convenient place independent of the propeller shafts, the turbine room being exactly like an Electric Power Station in a city, situated in the most advantageous place and distributing its power by cables to the places where the power is required. Another point is that the turbine room can be situated between two boiler rooms, so shortening the runs of the steam piping, and in these days of extra high pressures requiring very costly steel piping this is a great item, apart from the fact that the tremendous powers now

STIRLING-CASTLE

used call for such large steam pipes and of course the nearer each turbine is to the bank of boilers supplying it with steam, the better it is for the overall efficiency. Another advantage is the fact that in the case of a four propeller liner like *Normandie* with four main turbine-generators, any number of turbines can be used to propel the ship at the required speed by the simple method of switching. For instance two turbo sets could run all four motors at half speed or even two motors at half ship speed, which is a great advantage in the case of breakdowns, although steam turbine breakdowns are a very rare event. The turbine-generator sets can be run up to full speed for tests in dock without turning a propeller. No other form of drive can give this advantage, which very often means a great saving of money and time as even after an extensive overhaul a sea trial would not be necessary. The newer drive dispenses with the great heavy mechanical gearing that is necessary to bring the turbine speed down to propeller speed. The fact that no reverse turbines are necessary and that the turbo-sets always run in the same direction whatever direction the propulsion motors are required to travel in is another advantage. The first merchant vessels with this drive were built in the United States for the United States Shipping Board in 1918, they being the cargo vessels *Courageous* and *Defiance*, each of about 7,500 tons.

The first passenger liners being the *Pennsylvania, California* and *Virginia* built in 1928/9 for the American Line S.S. Corporation of New York, a branch of the International Mercantile Marine Company. They are of approximately 18,000 tons gross each.

In the British Isles the first electrically propelled ocean steamer was the *San Benito* built in 1923 for the United Fruit Company, and the first turbo-electric liner was the famous (P. & O.) liner *Viceroy of India* built in 1929 by Alexander Stephens & Sons at Glasgow. Altogether there have been about forty-eight ocean going ships built for mercantile service with this form of propulsion, and no doubt the success of the *Normandie* will increase the numbers considerably in the near future.

A further great change in ocean passenger travel since the War has been the decrease in the number of passengers carried by the great shipping lines due to the restrictions on emigration, although this has been partially counteracted by the great increase of travel by cabin and tourist classes of passengers and the great extension of popular cruises.

The great popularity of cabin class and tourist class travel has led to the conversion of many great liners to cabin class vessels, as well as the construction of new ships designed with these classes of accommodation, the greatest example of which is the decision of the Cunard White Star Line directors to put the splendid *Queen Mary* in this category, a decision which has caused great controversy in the North Atlantic shipping circles.

The outward design of liners has changed too, the counter stern giving place almost universally to the cruiser stern. Funnels have been reduced on the newer big liners from the four of pre-war days to three and in some cases to two, and the once common four-masted steamship has given place to the almost general use of two masts and in one or two cases one mast only has been fitted. Internally, luxury upon luxury has been added and now cafés, lidos and swimming baths are the general rule.

Up to the year 1914 Great Britain and Germany, with France just entering the lists, were the only serious rivals in building big express liners, but now there are six nations included in the list of owners of the sixty big ships covered by this volume, although Holland possesses only two of the total number with a third vessel of about 35,000 tons gross building. The United States in pre-war days only made one attempt at building a vessel of over the 20,000 ton mark, this being the *Minnesota* of 1904 which during the War, when the Atlantic Transport Line's fleet had either been lost or were exclusively on Government work, was transferred to the Atlantic Transport Company of West Virginia and put on the A.T.L. Atlantic service. Since the year 1928 there have been four vessels built in that country which come into the big ship class, the remainder of the American owned big ships being ex-German liners headed by the great *Leviathan*. The United States Lines are now having built two large liners, and Mr. Chapman, the head of that line, has already discussed plans for two giant ships of 100,000 tons gross, with accommodation for ten thousand tourist class passengers.

The greatest advance in the ownership of big liners has been made by Italy. In the year 1920 that country did not possess a single merchant ship of 20,000 tons or over and now she has a striking fleet of twelve splendid liners of this class headed by the great *Rex* and *Conte di Savoia.*

Germany has made a wonderful recovery since the year 1920 and although not reaching the proud position which she held in 1914, has built some fine ships, the record making *Bremen* and *Europa* on the North Atlantic and the *Cap Arcona* on the South Atlantic being the greatest examples.

Two other large ships have been built for the Mercantile service but not used on it, therefore are not included in the ships detailed in this volume. These are the *Justita* built for the Holland-Amerika Line as the *Statendam* by Harland & Wolff, Ltd., a vessel of nearly 35,000 tons gross. She was, however, taken over by the Admiralty on the outbreak of war and hurriedly completed as a transport and on the 25th of September, 1918, she was torpedoed and sank the following day. The other vessel was the Italian turbine steamer *Caracciolo*, a 25,000 ton vessel built at the Italian Government Dockyard at Castellmare in 1921, but no record of her being employed on mercantile work seems to exist.

In the year 1905 the White Star Line, pursuing their policy of building large and comfortable ships of moderate speed, received from the builders at Belfast the largest merchant ship in the world to date, the s.s. *Baltic*, a splendid liner of 23,881 tons gross.

She was the third of what later became known as the "White Star Big Four," her predecessors being the *Cedric* of 1904 and *Celtic* of 1902, and the fourth being the famous *Adriatic* of 1906 of which more will be said later.

S.S. *Baltic* became for some inexplicable reason the most popular of the four similar ships and coming unscathed through the War she had a long and proud record on the western ocean, ending her useful service by going to the ship-breakers in 1933.

BREMEN

She, like many another fine ship, would no doubt have had many more years of service, but the economic depression and the cutting down of emigration hastened her end.

Another big ship of 1905 was the North German Lloyd liner *Kaiserin Auguste Victoria* of 24,500 tons gross. She was not an express liner, being designed on the same lines as the White Star big ships, with large passenger carrying capacity and moderate speed. She was a very profitable ship for her owners and was kept fully employed until August, 1914, when she was in port in Germany and remained tied up throughout the War, and in 1919 was ceded to Great Britain under the Treaty of Versailles and after some miscellaneous duties for the Shipping Controller under Cunard Line management was sold to the Canadian Pacific Railway Company.

Her new owners had her completely refitted and with alterations giving her a gross tonnage of 25,160 tons she was renamed *Empress of Scotland*, being very useful on various services and on cruising, and was finally sold to the shipbreakers in 1934.

The White Star Liner *Adriatic* was the only great ship of the year 1906, the fourth of the "White Star Big Four" to go into service, having a gross tonnage of 24,679 she was therefore slightly larger than the *Kaiserin Auguste Victoria* and was the largest ship in the world to date. In design she was a larger edition than her consorts and always was a very popular vessel on the Atlantic, during the War earning the title of "Queen of the Munition Fleet." She gave her owners a long and profitable service, going to the scrappers in 1934, and so ended the last of the famous four ships which had carried thousands of pleasure seekers and business people in safety over the treacherous Atlantic besides carrying hundreds and hundreds of thousands of emigrants from Europe to the lands of greater opportunity in the west.

The year 1907 will never be forgotten as the year of the inception of the famous Cunarders *Lusitania* and *Mauretania*. They, as befitted their importance, had the year to themselves as far as the big ships were concerned. These great and now historic vessels were such an advance in naval architecture and engineering science that they marked a new stage in the history of the world's mercantile marine. The enterprising and far seeing Directors of the Cunard Steamship Company, true to the traditions of their race, and backed by the British Government, gave their competitors such a sweeping blow by the size and speed of the famous pair that it was some time before either record was broken.

The *Lusitania* arrived from her builders, Messrs. John Brown & Co. Ltd., in October, 1907, after a great send off by the people of the Clyde district. The whole of the Merseyside population and thousands of visitors welcomed her at Liverpool, her home port, and shortly afterwards she left on her maiden voyage for New York amid general acclamation, a picture of proud majesty, speed and power. She had a great reception in New York, having on her first trip

QUEEN MARY

lowered the Atlantic record in very bad weather, this bringing the coveted Blue Riband of the Atlantic back to Britain after a stay of ten years in Germany. Her record was lowered only by her sister ship which arrived from Tyneside shortly afterwards, having been constructed by Messrs. Swan, Hunter & Wigham Richardson, Ltd.

On November 16th, the stately and beautiful *Mauretania* left Liverpool on her maiden voyage, taking her place alongside her sister ship and the two older but still famous record makers *Lucania* and *Campania*, the four vessels maintaining a weekly express service until the *Lucania* unfortunately was burned out and scuttled in Huskisson Dock, Liverpool, during the year 1909, but was raised and later sold to the scrappers. The express service was maintained by the three ships, the wonderful *Campania* keeping the three-weekly schedule with her larger and faster consorts until the advent of the *Aquitania*, in 1913.

Mauretania had no difficulty in lowering her sister ship's record and the two splendid vessels continued to make record after record, although the *Mauretania* proved herself always slightly the faster of the two and she held the Blue Riband of the Atlantic for twenty-two years, a feat never before accomplished and one that will probably never be again performed. The *full story of this great ship is given in Mr. Gerald Aylmer's splendid little book "Mauretania."*

The unfortunate *Lusitania* met her untimely end due to enemy action in May, 1915, taking with her one thousand one hundred and ninety-eight lives. The story of her tragic end has been told by many far abler pens than mine so no more will be said here of the awful tragedy.

Mauretania came through the War without a blemish, having instead added new honours to her glory. After paying off she was refitted and converted to an oil burner, and then proceeded to make more record trips. In 1929 she made the best day's run of her career at an average speed of 27.48 knots and she finished the voyage with a record making spurt on the 106 miles course between Eddystone lighthouse and Cherbourg at a wonderful average speed of 29.7 knots, the fastest recorded speed for her or any other merchant ship up to date. Not content with this, the grand Old Lady of the Seas made another record in 1933. When returning to New York from a West Indian cruise she left Havana on July 19th, and by noon on the 20th she had travelled 603 miles at an average of 27.78 knots, including one 112 mile stretch at actually 32 knots, she being then twenty-two years old. She continued in service until 1935 when her maintenance costs getting too high, she was sold to the shipbreakers in July, 1935. Her departure from Southampton on her last sad voyage to Rosyth was broadcast by the British Broadcasting Corporation and the good old ship blew her farewell with her syren to millions of listeners. The whole nation felt a personal loss and during her last voyage up the East Coast she was saluted by hundreds of craft of all kinds and when off the Tyne, the place of her launch she was hove to, and a deputation headed by the Mayor of Newcastle came on board to say farewell officially to the grand old ship. All kinds of suggestions were put forward to keep her intact but without avail and she is now nothing more than a lifeless mass of broken steel.

Holland in 1908 entered the lists of big ship-owning countries with the fine steamship *Rotterdam* of 24,159 tons gross, built at Belfast by the famous Harland & Wolff Company for the Holland-Amerika Line. She is a typical H. & W.

INTRODUCTION

job and her arrival and first departure from Rotterdam were the scenes of great enthusiasm. She, like her White Star prototypes, is a roomy comfortable ship with a medium speed and a fine sea boat, very popular with American-Dutch travellers and also on cruising. She is still in service and was the largest Dutch Liner for twenty-one years.

In this same year, 1908, Germany added another fine liner named *George Washington* to her mercantile marine and while not a record maker either in size or speed, being of 25,570 tons gross, she proved a valuable ship to her owners, the North German Lloyd Company, and was the largest vessel they owned until the coming out of the *Columbus* in 1924. She again was a big passenger carrier being specially built with large emigrant accommodation and had a successful career until 1914, when on the outbreak of war she was interned by the United States Government, and in 1917 became a U.S. armed auxiliary cruiser, her appropriate name not being changed by the U.S. Navy Department. After the Armistice she was run for the United States Shipping Board by the United American Mail Line and later by the United States Lines. Apparently she has come to the end of her usefulness and has been laid up in Chesapeake Bay since September, 1932.

The year 1909 was a blank year as regards the construction of big ships but plans were maturing and in 1910 The Cie. Generale Transatlantique (the French Line) launched their fine big ship named *France*, a beauty of 23,769 tons gross. She was the largest French owned liner until the *Paris* of 1920 and in external appearance was very like a smaller edition of the famous Cunard pair. The French nation was exceedingly proud of their latest and largest luxury liner bearing the name of their country.

The White Star determined not to be outdone on the question of size, and still pursuing their policy of big, moderate speed, roomy vessels, decided to build two record breakers to eclipse the famous Cunarders in size, if not speed, and in 1911, the first of these ships came out of the builder's yard at Belfast. This was the *Olympic*, a huge vessel of over 46,000 tons gross, almost 50 per cent larger than the famous Cunard pair, arousing the greatest interest in the shipping world and creating world-wide interest. Although not possessing the speed of the two Cunard greyhounds, she had beautiful lines, and was a magnificently spacious ship. Her decorations and the luxury of her appointments made her indeed a floating palace, and a great credit to her designers, builders and owners.

She was followed by her unfortunate sister ship *Titanic* in 1912, whose tragic and uncompleted maiden voyage will never be forgotten, it being the most appalling tragedy that the world's merchant marine ever suffered in times of peace. She was the replica of her sister ship, the only variations being in her decorations, etc.

"Old Reliable," as the *Olympic* became known during the War, had a wonderful and profitable life, going to the scrappers shortly after *Mauretania* in 1935, and she is the largest liner yet to reach such a fate. Her omission from the sailing lists leaves a great gap, and she will be missed on both sides of the Atlantic.

NORMANDIE
By courtesy of the French Line

In this same year (1912) the Hamburg-Amerika Line had launched at the Vulcan Yard a still larger vessel. She came into service in 1913 and was named *Imperator*. The largest ship yet to sail the seas, she was indeed an Emperor of the Ocean, but is now better known as the *Berengaria* of the Cunard White Star Line. This great and beautiful ship reached the previously unheard-of tonnage of over 52,000 tons gross, and an overall length of 919 ft., and to-day she is the fourth ship in size, including *Normandie* and *Queen Mary*.

The Hamburg Company excelled themselves in her artistic decorations and luxurious furnishings, and her great, spacious public rooms seemed to be the last word in floating palaces. She was in Hamburg when the War broke out, and was due to sail for New York, but the sailing was cancelled and she remained in port until she was ceded to Great Britain by the Versailles Treaty and duly handed over to the British Shipping Controller, who sold her to the Cunard Line to replace the lost *Lusitania*.

The great ship of the year 1913 was the *Aquitania*, a larger edition of *Mauretania* in appearance, but of 45,647 tons gross, with an overall length of 901 ft. She is a more spacious ship than her Cunard predecessors, although of a more moderate speed, but being built without any Government assistance, the Company had to design her with a view to luxurious travel with economy of operation. She is reputed to have carried more travellers across the Atlantic than any other liner, and she has proved to be an entirely reliable and economical vessel. After twenty-two years of service she is still popular and has a great following amongst regular trans-atlantic passengers, and is still going strong. Until the advent of the *Queen Mary's* sister ship she will maintain the weekly Southampton-New York service with the *Queen Mary* and *Berengaria*. What a noble trio they make!

The fateful year in the world's history (1914) saw the second of the three Hamburg-Amerika Line's huge liners in service. This was the *Vaterland*, now known as *Leviathan* of the United States Lines. She was longer and of even greater tonnage than the *Imperator* as originally built, but since she was taken over by the United States Government in 1917, has been so altered by a number of re-fits that there has been considerable confusion as to her actual size. The fact remains, however, that when she went on service, she was the largest ship in the world. She was on her third trans-atlantic trip, and when, on the fateful August 4th, 1914, she was in New York, the German authorities, not wishing to risk her capture by the allied naval forces, ordered her to remain in port where, after the usual time allowance had expired, she was interned.

In 1917, having been seized by the United States Government as a transport, a service which she well performed, carrying more troops than any other ship ever known, she carried as many troops as ten thousand at a time, plus a large crew, and she was known to American soldiers as "Levi Nathan." Since the Armistice, she has proved something of a white elephant, and it has been reported that she has cost over £12,000,000 to the American Government and the companies running her since 1919. She had her tonnage increased during one of her re-fits, giving her a larger tonnage than the *Majestic*, although she was 7 ft. shorter. This was apparently to enable her to be advertised as the world's largest liner; this increase in tonnage has, it is estimated, cost her owners some £100,000 in increased pilot, harbour and dock dues.

The next largest vessel of the year 1914 was the White Star Liner *Britannic*,

INTRODUCTION

a great ship of 48,156 tons gross. The largest British built liner prior to the *Queen Mary*, she was intended to replace the ill-fated *Titanic* as consort to the *Olympic*, being built on generally the same lines as her predecessors only slightly larger. Being requisitioned by the British Admiralty before being handed over by the builders she never appeared on the service she was built for. Commissioned as a Hospital ship and sent out to the Eastern Mediterranean for service with the Dardanelles Expeditionary Force she was unfortunately sunk by enemy action in 1916 when in the Aegean Sea, twenty-one of her crew and nine hospital ratings being killed. *Britannic* was less in size than the big Hamburg-Amerika Liners but she was a beautiful ship with four large funnels like her intended consort *Olympic* and would have been as luxurious as any ship on the ocean. Like the other White Star Liners she was built at Belfast by Messrs. Harland & Wolff, Ltd., who were building at the same time a fine 27,000 tonner for the Red Star Line.

This ship like many others in the shipbuilders' hands during that time of stress was left unfinished owing to the urgencies of Naval work, but when the need became urgent for mercantile tonnage for transport and other urgent national duties, she was hurriedly partially completed as a large cargo carrier and used under White Star Line management as the *Belgic*. In 1920 she was completed to the original plans and went to the Red Star Line under her intended name of *Belgenland*, being registered under British registry and flag by Messrs. F. Leyland & Co., Ltd., of Liverpool.

Belgenland was employed on the Antwerp—New York service of the International Mercantile Marine Company's Red Star Line for many years. During a strike at Antwerp docks she was diverted to London, being the largest ship to dock in the Port of London until in 1935 the Cunard-White Star Liners *Britannic* and *Georgic* were put on the London service.

When the Atlantic Transport Liners *Minnewaska* and *Minnetonka* were transferred to the Red Star service, *Belgenland* was used as a cruising ship, making a number of cruises from London, and she became a regular feature in London River off Gravesend and in Tilbury Docks. When the International Mercantile Marine Company decided to close down their European interests and only employ vessels of American registry on their American lines they transferred *Belgenland* to the Atlantic Transport Company of West Virginia for the Panama Pacific service and renamed her *Columbia*. She was given an extensive refit at Tilbury and her name and registry were changed before she sailed for New York under the American flag on January 10th, 1935, commanded by Captain Jensen, late of the U.S. Liner *President Roosevelt*. She was a big loss to London following the loss sustained by the closing down of the Atlantic Transport Line.

War expediences demanding either naval craft or cargo vessels prevented the building of any other large liners during 1914/1918, but a number of partially finished vessels in this class were lying unfinished in German yards and one in France. Amongst these were the third of the

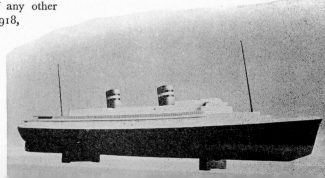

NIEUW AMSTERDAM

Hamburg-Amerika Line's giants which had been launched and named *Bismarck*; others were the N.D.L. Liner *Columbus* and the Hamburg Sud Amerika Liner *Cap Polonio*. The French vessel was lying at St. Nazaire and she was the now famous *Paris* of the Cie. Generale Transatlantique.

The year 1915 brought the terrible loss of the *Lusitania* on May 7th, a tragedy which shocked the world and which probably was the main cause of changing the American attitude to the War and so indirectly was the cause of the United States entering into the World War. The great and noble ship took down with her a death roll that was only second to the great loss in the *Titanic*.

The year 1916 brought the tragic loss of the *Britannic* as already mentioned.

The World's Mercantile Marine was in 1920 busily engaged in getting back to its peace time stride, although times were not yet normal, the big event of the year regarding the big ships was the surrender of the big German liners. *Bismarck* the third and last of the Hamburg-Amerika Line's giants was completed and handed over to the British Shipping Controller who disposed of her to the White Star Line to replace the lost *Britannic*. She, the largest and probably the most luxurious ship in the world, was re-named by her new owners very appropriately *Majestic*, and was placed on the Southampton–New York run, on which she remained until 1936, she has now been bought by the Admiralty for use as a training ship, after refitting extensively at Rosyth. *Majestic* has proved a splendid vessel and has a great following on the Atlantic; in 1923 she was converted to oil burning and this improved her average speed, for after the conversion she made a crossing at the good average of 24·76 knots. Herr Albert Ballin who planned the three great Hamburg-Amerikan ships, died before his plans were completed. He little thought when making his plans that all three of his great ships would sail under other flags than that of the famous H.A.P.A.G., but such are the fortunes of war.

The *Columbus* was also completed in Germany and likewise handed over to the British Shipping Controller, going to the White Star Line later who re-named her *Homeric* after the great poet, although a name that is different from the usual White Star style. She is a fine ship of over 34,000 tons gross and has done good work for her owners on the North Atlantic run and perhaps more especially as a cruising liner. She was the largest ship ever ordered by the famous Bremen Line prior to the war and the N.D.L. replaced her in 1924 with a vessel of very similar design which they also named *Columbus*. The *Homeric* was sold in 1936 to Thos. W. Ward, Ltd., Sheffield, for breaking up.

France made her second contribution to the world's fleet of big ships in 1921 by the completion and placing in service of the great *Paris* so aptly named, as the then largest ship of the country's mercantile fleet, after the capital city. She is a beautiful ship of 34,500 tons gross, and like the big ships ordered by the Hamburg Company she has three funnels in place of the big ships' usual four which has become so general after the advent of the *Lusitania* and *Mauretania*.

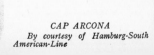

CAP ARCONA
By courtesy of Hamburg-South
American-Line

INTRODUCTION

Paris soon made a great name for herself on the Atlantic, being known as the " Aristocrat of Liners," her artistic decorations and superb public rooms being, it seemed, the last word in style and good taste.

Italy which had received from the builders on the Tyne a fine big liner named *Giulo Cesare* in 1921, a vessel which put Italy in the list of owners of big ships, put a second big liner in commission in 1923. Larger than the first the *Duilio* is 23,635 tons gross. She was built in Italy, being the first big liner to be built in that country, meaning by big liner one of over 20,000 tons gross.

Previous to the war Italy had been content to run her merchant marine with foreign built and very often second hand tonnage, but now she possesses some of the finest ships afloat, and a good start was made with *Duilio* and her consort which are as fine a pair of ships as any country would be proud to possess.

The Atlantic Transport Line of London having suffered tremendous war losses had maintained their service with the chartered *Manchuria* and *Mongolia*, together with the transferred *Minnesota*, all these three being ships of American registry. In 1923 they commenced to rebuild their fleet with the ordering of a pair a fine ships of nearly 22,000 tons gross from Messrs. Harland & Wolff, Ltd. These fine steamships, which incidentally were the largest cargo carriers ever built, had splendid first class only accommodation. Named with traditional names of the line, *Minnetonka* and *Minnewaska* they soon became popular on the London–New York service and it was a great loss to London when they were transferred to the Red Star Antwerp–New York service. In 1933 they were, after being laid up some time, sold to the shipbreakers, the breaking up of such a fine pair of practically new and large ships creating a record, as never before had such ships met such an early fate. In this same year, 1923, the North German Lloyd Company brought out their new *Columbus*, a beautiful two-funnelled ship of 32,565 tons gross, built as before stated to replace the loss of the previous *Columbus* now *Homeric*. She was the first big post-war liner built for the historic Bremen Company and is equipped, decorated and furnished on the usual lavish standard of the line. Being of somewhat similar design to the previous ship she is slightly smaller and her funnels are shorter giving her a more modern appearance.

The Italians in 1925 added another fine liner to their fleet in the *Conte di Biancamano* built by Sir William Beardmore & Co., Ltd., at Glasgow for the Genoa–New York service. A fine ship of nearly 25,000 tons gross, she has a large accommodation for passengers. The Italian Government found her very useful for trooping to East Africa in 1935.

The Hamburg–Amerika Line added to their fleet this same year the *Hamburg*, a vessel of over 22,000 tons gross, being an improvement on the Albert Ballin class built in 1923, equipped in the usual high standard of the line.

On the South American route the Royal Mail Steam Packet Co., now the Royal Mail Lines, came into the big ship owning class by building their first liner of over 20,000 tons gross, the motor ship *Asturias*, a beautiful and luxurious vessel

NEW YORK
By courtesy of Hamburg-Amerika Line.

of over 21,000 tons gross, since altered to over 22,000 tons gross. Her advent marks a new era for ships on the South Atlantic, the Royal Mail Company being the oldest steamer line in this trade. The company was, however, as will be seen later, to face big competition from continental lines in the near future.

The vessel of 1926 was the great French liner *Ile de France*, in which the very zenith of luxury seemed to have been reached. She is entirely modern in her decorative schemes and a great ship of 43,000 tons gross; the pride of France until she was eclipsed by the mighty *Normandie* in 1935. She is as beautiful a ship as her name, and is one of the most popular liners on the Atlantic especially with American visitors to Europe. Her appointments are so essentially French that they give the American traveller the impression of being in France the moment he steps on board in New York.

Italy, still pressing forward in big ship owning, had built in Italy in the same year the 32,500 tons gross liner *Roma*, the largest Italian liner to date. She is a fine example of naval architecture and is fitted with every modern refinement and convenience for the comfort of her passengers. In Britain the Royal Mail Company added the second of their big motor vessels to their South American Fleet by the placing in service of the m.s. *Alcantara*, a sister ship to the *Asturias*, which maintain the Line's Southampton–South America service with the older *Almanzora* and *Arlanza*. In the face of competition of faster ships on this run the Company later had these two vessels speeded up by the removing of their engines and the installation of steam turbines and with other alterations their tonnage was increased to over the 22,000 tons gross mark.

The year 1927 was essentially Italy's year by the placing in service of the world's largest Motor Liner *Augustus*, of 32,650 tons gross, a sister ship to *Roma*. except as to engines, making a very fine pair of ships that have been very successful.

The next Italian effort of the year being the building, also in Italy, of the *Conte Grande* of 25,600 tons gross, and of the Motor Liner *Saturnia* of nearly 24,000 tons gross. The building of these large ships definitely put Italy amongst the big ship-owning nations and so rapid had been her advance that in 1935 she had no less than twelve large liners of over 20,000 tons gross, being only second to Great Britain in numbers of big liners.

In Germany the same year the Hamburg–Amerika Line placed in service the *New York*, a sister to the *Hamburg*, bringing the number of the line's big ships up to six. She and her post war sisters are not very handsome vessels to look at as regards their external design, but internally they uphold the traditions of the line for well appointed passenger accommodation. Germany's best effort of the year was the great South American Liner *Cap Arcona*, built for the Hamburg Sud Amerika Line, which created a record for size and speed on this route, and the largest liner the company have owned. She is a worthy vessel to follow the traditions of the famous *Cap Trafalgar* and the *Cap Polonio*. The advent of this ship of 27,500 tons gross made the new distinction for the port of Hamburg in the fact that its largest vessel was sailing to a port other than New York.

The largest liner to be built and placed in service in 1928 was the Canadian Pacific Line's *Empress of Japan*, a 26,000 ton ship of superb lines and equipment. She was placed on the Pacific run alongside the *Empress of Canada* and her predecessors, and is the largest and fastest liner to be employed regularly on the

Pacific Ocean. A beautiful ship with her gleaming white hull and upper works and three huge yellow funnels. Her first arrival at Vancouver was welcomed by admiring crowds of people and she received quite an ovation when leaving on her initial service voyage. The Italians added another large motor driven liner to their fleet during the same year in the *Vulcania*, a sister ship and a replica of the *Saturnia*.

The year 1929 was an epoch-making year by the advent of the great record-making and largest post war liners to be built to date. The North German Lloyd Company gave their traditional names of *Bremen* and *Europa* to these great vessels, and immediately they entered service they made records, the *Bremen* first, for the *Europa* was unfortunately delayed during fitting out at Hamburg by a disastrous fire which broke out in her almost finished passenger accommodation. *Bremen* is slightly the larger of the two and has proved to be also the faster, and has a tonnage of 51,656 tons gross. The German people all the world over hailed her advent on the Atlantic with delight and rightly felt that the German Mercantile Marine was coming back to its former honoured position by possessing such a superb pair of vessels. On the arrival of the *Bremen* at New York on her maiden voyage she was received by the Mayor and Aldermen of the City, and the German Societies of New York presented the ship with an engraved plaque which has been fixed in a prominent position on board. The *Bremen* lifted the Blue Riband of the Atlantic from the *Mauretania*, after the latter ship had held it for twenty-two years. The *Europa* improved on *Bremen's* record but later the *Bremen* settled down and regained the record from her sister ship, keeping the record until it was again won in 1932, this time by Italy, the newest rivals in the race, with the magnificent *Rex*. The North German Lloyd pair have proved highly successful in service, their wonderful passenger accommodation and modern luxury taking thousands of passengers from the older liners. In appearance they are very modern with two short funnels and streamlined hull. Undoubtedly they are two of the finest ships ever built and many people consider them the most beautiful ships afloat.

The next largest ship of the year was the almost 30,000 ton *Statendam*, of the Holland–America Line, the largest Dutch liner to date. This fine vessel had the distinction of being built in two countries. The contract was placed with Messrs. Harland & Wolff, Ltd., and she was launched and partially finished by them. Work was held up and finally she was taken to Holland and finished off at Wilton's shipyard at Rotterdam. She is known as " Queen of the Spotless Fleet," and has earned well deserved popularity. Her decorations and furnishings and the whole artistic scheme are essentially Dutch in a very beautiful way.

Another liner of a new and striking design which came out this same year was the motor ship *Lafayette*, the first large French motor vessel. She is of 25,178 tons gross, and made a big addition to the French Line's cabin class fleet. She is very richly appointed and her public rooms are very modern and elegant. Her exterior design is notable for her one huge funnel and one mast.

In the year 1930 the largest ship to go into commission was the ill-fated *L'Atlantique* of the Cie. Sud Atlantique, being the largest liner yet to be built for the South American trade; she was of 40,000 tons gross, and her coming out created quite a furore in the shipping world. Her serviceable life was, however, not to be long duration, she being practically destroyed by fire in the

English Channel on January 4th, 1933. Fortunately no passengers were on board at the time of the tragic occurrence and only a skeleton crew, she being on her way from Bordeaux to Havre for a refit. The question of whether she was a total loss or was repairable has been the cause of much litigation in the French courts, the English underwriters contending that she could be put in her former condition for less than the total loss insured value.

The next largest liner of the year was from the yard of Messrs. Harland & Wolff, Ltd., and was the largest motor vessel as yet constructed in a British yard. She is of 26,943 tons gross, and was given by her owners, the White Star Line, the historic name of *Britannic* in honour of previous ships bearing the patriotic name. A magnificent vessel with two squat funnels and with all the latest in modern equipment and beautiful appointments, offering cabin class passengers accommodation and comfort that would have been unheard of for saloon passengers not so very long ago. With her sister ship *Georgic* she was transferred to the London–Boston and New York service for the summer of 1935, and they are the largest pair of liners to have as yet docked in the port of London.

America provided the next large ship of the year by placing in service the first of a fine pair of turbo-electric liners built for the Dollar Line of San Francisco, an old established Californian company going back to sailing ship days and founded by that well-known shipping owner Robert Dollar, a Scotsman who settled on the Pacific coast. The new ship named *President Hoover* is of nearly 22,000 tons gross, and is the largest turbo-electric liner to date, being a fine and luxurious vessel engaged on the San Francisco–Panama and New York service.

The year 1931 brought Britain's post war " Wonder Ship," the largest vessel to be built in the British Isles since the *Britannic* of 1914, of 42,348 tons gross. Built for the enterprising Canadian Pacific Line, who named her *Empress of Britain*, thus carrying on the name of an earlier vessel of the fleet, sister to the ill-fated *Empress of Ireland*, which was so tragically sunk in 1914 in the St. Lawrence River. This great and beautiful vessel is the largest, fastest and most luxurious ever to be put on the Canadian service and she has made herself world renown for her successful round the world cruises, being the largest vessel to pass through the Suez and Panama Canals. Launched by the Duke of Windsor when he was the Prince of Wales in 1930 she had a great send-off and her first appearance in the St. Lawrence River caused the greatest enthusiasm amongst the Canadian people.

The second largest liner of 1931 was the first of the two largest and most luxurious liners yet to be built in the United States is the *Manhattan* of the United States Lines, a 24,000 tons gross vessel. Not so large as the White Star motor ship of the previous year they vie with each other for the splendid cabin class accommodation, which is the highest class they carry. Quite apart from the two ships mentioned above 1931 was the year of the turbo-electric liner, no less than three large liners with this form of propulsion drive appearing, two British and one American. It

CONTE DI SAVOIA

is remarkable how little attention other countries have given this form of drive, Germany lagging behind as she did when steam turbines were introduced did not build any liners with this the newest form of propulsion until 1934, when two 18,000 ton liners were ordered for the North German Lloyd far eastern service in association with the Hansa Company led by the *Schornhorst*. Of the other countries only France has used this form of drive for a big ship and then she went all out for it with the mighty *Normandie*.

The largest turbo-electric ship of the year is the *Strathnaver*, of 22,500 tons gross, built at Barrow for the P. & O. Company. The first of the already popular " Two White Sisters " of the line, with their three large yellow funnels and their white hulls these splendid and essentially modern looking vessels have already made history on the London–India and Australian trade. The other British turbo-electric vessel being the *Monarch of Bermuda*, also built at Barrow by Messrs. Vickers, Armstrongs, Ltd. With her sister ship the *Queen of Bermuda* these fine turbo-electric liners, the largest ships owned by Messrs. Furness, Withy & Co., Ltd., of Liverpool, and London, maintain a service between New York and Bermuda. They are the largest vessels to be ever employed on such a short run. So handsome and luxurious are they that they soon became known as " The Millionaires' Ships."

Italy in the year 1932 put into service their two record-making super liners *Rex* and *Conte di Savoia*, a regal and beautiful pair of ships of 51,000 and 48,900 tons gross respectively. The *Rex* was the first out but was unfortunate on her maiden voyage, having turbine trouble which delayed her at Gibraltar, but in August, 1933, she made a record trip across the Atlantic, winning the Blue Riband of the Atlantic from the N.D.L. *Bremen*, this being the first time any nation other than British, American or German has held the coveted trophy. The *Conte di Savoia* proved slightly slower than her sister ship. The appointments of these wonderful vessels are most sumptuous and distinguished. They are the largest vessels yet to be built in any country other than Great Britain and Ireland, Germany or France, and the Italian nation are justly proud of owning such a great pair of ships.

The French Line added to their fleet another fine cabin class liner in 1932 named *Champlain*, a sister ship to the *Lafayette* except as to engines and small details. She is a turbine driven ship and readily distinguishable by having a smoke deflecting cap fitted to her funnel. They are a splendid pair and their decorations and furnishings have a charm all their own.

This same year the second big motor ship for the White Star Line came out, the already mentioned *Georgic*, similar to the *Britannic* only of slightly larger tonnage.

The P. & O. Company added the second of the " White Sisters " to their fleet this same year; she is the *Strathaird*, and is a replica of her sister ship. These splendid turbo-electric vessels have been highly successful and they steam along as quietly and with as little vibration as a sailing vessel. They are exceedingly popular on the Indian and Australian runs as well as on cruising work, and they arouse the keenest interest wherever they go.

In the United States the second big cabin class liner appeared in the fleet of the United States Lines, bearing the historic name of *Washington*. She is practically indistinguishable from her sister ship *Manhattan*.

In 1932 the second big Dollar Liner *President Coolidge* also came in service, and like her sister ship she is turbo-electric.

The two greatest maritime events of the year 1932 were, however, the laying down of the two super Atlantic liners *Queen Mary* and *Normandie*, the former at Clydebank and the latter at St. Nazaire, where she was launched on October 29th.

The year also saw the end of a number of great liners, *Carmania*, *Caronia*, *Cedric* and *America*, all going to the scrappers.

Messrs. Furness, Withy & Co., in the year 1933, accepted delivery from the builders Messrs. Vickers, Armstrongs, Ltd., of Barrow, of their second turbo-electric vessel the *Queen of Bermuda*, a ship as royal as her name. This great and luxurious 22,424 ton liner was built in the record time of fourteen months to replace the motor ship *Bermuda* lost by fire in Belfast where she was refitting after a fire at Bermuda. During the absence of a consort for the *Monarch of Bermuda* the Cunarder *Franconia* was chartered until the arrival of the *Queen of Bermuda*.

1933 also saw the end of three large liners, the *Baltic* and *France* going to the scrappers, and as already mentioned the loss by fire of the *L'Atlantique*.

The year 1934 was a blank year as regards placing in service of any large liners, but after being held up for some time work was resumed on the *Queen Mary*, and the whole nation was thrilled when on September 26th, H.M. Queen Mary in the presence of H.M. King George V, gave her own name to the great vessel, afterwards successfully launching her. Thousands of visitors invaded the Clydeside area and the whole district had a day's holiday for the historic event.

In this year four fine big liners went to the scrappers, these being the *Empress of Scotland*, ex-*Kaiserin Auguste Victoria*, the fine old *Adriatic*, and London's two largest liners, *Minnetonka* and *Minnewaska*.

1935 saw the completion and the placing in service of the epoch making super liner *Normandie* of the French Line, a giant of nearly 80,000 tons gross, the most superbly appointed and artistically decorated luxury liner yet to sail the seas. With her gigantic power plant and four huge electric motors driving her great propellers she had no difficulty in lifting the Blue Riband of the Atlantic on her first voyage, from the Italian Liner *Rex*. Thus in a very short time the trophy passed from Britain to Germany on to Italy, then to France.

The whole of the French people were delighted at the success of their great ship and her advent dwarfed all maritime events of the year.

In Britain some smaller but quite interesting vessels were delivered to their respective owners; the Orient Line improved on their well-known *Orama* class with the new *Orion*, a fine ship of over 23,000 tons gross, an unusual feature of her for a ship of this line being the fitting of only one funnel and one mast, she is a great ship and has already been cruising and made several trips to Australia and back very successfully. A very similar ship by the same builders, Messrs. Vickers, Armstrongs, Ltd., is the

STATENDAM
By courtesy of Holland-America Line.

INTRODUCTION

latest P. & O. liner *Strathmore*, also a very beautiful and graceful ship, she is slightly faster than the *Orion* and if anything even more luxurious. *Strathmore* has her hull painted white and her funnel yellow like her predecessors the " Two White Sisters." The next big liner to be launched was the *Stirling Castle*, a 25,000 ton motor liner for the Union–Castle Steamship Company's mail service from Southampton to South Africa and is an improvement on the *Winchester* and *Warwick Castles*. A sister ship, the *Athlone Castle*, was launched on November 18th, by H.R.H. Princess Alice, Countess of Athlone. These two new ships mark another advance in size on the South African run.

In June, the shiplovers of all the world over were sorry to hear of the sale to the scrappers of " Grand Old Lady of the Seas," the *Mauretania*, and she left Southampton on her last voyage on July 1st. In October, " Old Reliable," otherwise the *Olympic*, followed in her wake up the East Coast to Jarrow-on-Tyne for breaking up; thus ended the usefulness of two fine old record makers, but efficiency and progress must take precedence over sentiment. These two famous ships have worn the Blue Ensign through peace and war, storm and calm, sunshine and gloom, from what now seems that remote time " before the war," and now their time is over and new wonders take their places, the skill of the naval architects, marine engineers and craftsmen will go on turning out wonder after wonder until perhaps one day in the remote future a new form of transport will take the place of these giants of the seas.

The historic *Cap Polonio* was also sent to the scrappers during the year to the disappointment of the Hamburg people to whom she meant so much.

The great *Majestic* has escaped the scrappers; she being purchased by the Admiralty for use as a training ship for boys entering the Navy.

1936. The *Queen Mary* gained the Blue Riband by her crossing from west to east in three days 23 hours 57 minutes at an average speed of 30.63 knots.

So progress marches on and may the World's Mercantile Marine prosper and its fine seamen of all maritime nations sail the seven seas at peace with each other in their persistent fight with the awful forces of nature.

CHAMPLAIN
By courtesy of the French Line

GIANT LINERS OF THE WORLD

EXPLANATIONS OF ABBREVIATIONS
USED IN TEXT

Gross or register tonnage .	Cubic feet capacity of all enclosed space divided by 100.
Nat. & Port . . .	Country and port of registry.
Lg.	Length o.a.—overall, b.p.—between perpendiculars.
Depth	Depth of vessel. Drt. draught at normal load.
Nor. Spd. . . .	Normal service speed.
Knots	1 nautical mile per hour, or 1·1515 land miles per hour.
Dimensions . . .	Dimensions of hull.
S.H.P.	Shaft horse-power.
B.H.P.	Brake horse-power.
I.H.P.	Indicated horse-power.
F.D.	Forced draught to furnaces.
S.H.	Super heated steam to temperature given.
Trip. ex. . . .	Triple expansion, reciprocating steam engines.
Quad. ex. . . .	Quadruple expansion, reciprocating steam engines.
Cyls.	Cylinders in reciprocating steam or motor engines.
S.A.	Single-acting, applied to Diesel motor engines.
D.A.	Double-acting, applied to Diesel motor engines.
2 st.	Two-stroke, applied to Diesel motor engines.
4 st.	Four-stroke, applied to Diesel motor engines.

The tonnages given must not be taken as being perfectly accurate, as they change very frequently by a small amount, at each refit and re-measurement.

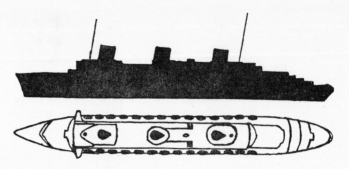

OWNERS:	Compagnie Generale Transatlantique. (The French Line.)
SERVICE:	Havre–New York.
NAT. & PORT:	French. Havre.
BUILDERS:	Soc. des. Ch. & Atliers de St. Nazaire, Penhoet, France, 1935.
TONNAGE:	Originally 79,280 tons gross, now 82,779 tons gross.
DIMENSIONS:	1,029 ft. lg. o.a. x 119 ft. beam. 220 ft. from water line to tip of forward funnel. 8 passenger decks.
ENGINES:	4 sets of steam turbine-generators, 4 Electric motors on screw shafts. 160,000 s.h.p. Quad. screw. Normal speed 30 knots.
BOILERS:	29 Sulzer mono-tube, water tube boilers, 400 lbs. stm. pr. 660 deg. super heat. Oil Fuel.
EL. LT. & PWR.:	Turbo-generators totalling 13,200 k.w. 40,000 lights. 770 telephone lines. Kitchen contains an electric cooker 55 ft. long.
PAINTWORK:	Black hull, red boot-topping, white upper works, red funnels with black tops.
COMPLEMENT:	2,000 pass., 448 1st class cabins, 40 with private open air terraces, 4 super suites-de-luxe, 10 other suites-de-luxe. Officers and Crew, 1,300.

Normandie is characteristically a French ship, but the two hemispheres have been called upon for rare and exquisite woods, enchantments in lacquer and glass, and fabrics and metal . . . rich treasures of tapestry, porcelain, silver art; 82,779 tons of beauty and comfort, the latest amazing material expression of man's daring imagination and of inexhaustible engineering experience. Her spacious salons, lofty dining saloon, wonderful regal stairway of gleaming marble with a bronze figure symbolizing Normandy at its crest, theatre salon with its fully-equipped stage, salon des dames, galerie salon, chapel, cafe-grill terrace, swimming pool 100 ft. long by 30 ft. wide, bridge rooms, smoke rooms, bars, and private suites are all too marvellous to be described in this small book as volumes could be written on their amazing luzury, comfort and beauty. Cost said to be £6,000,000.

1932, Oct. 29th. Launched. Launching weight 30,500 tons.

1935, Apr. Steam trials, she made 31·9 knots over several miles.

1935, May 20th. Maiden voyage commenced, Havre to New York, time between Southampton and Ambrose Light being 107 hrs. 33 mins., average speed of 29·68 knots on the return voyage she beat all records by 12 hrs. 47 mins., 4 days, 3 hrs. 28 mins., best day's run at average on 30·91 knots. On the voyage she did a speed of over 31 knots for several hours. She thus won the Atlantic Blue Riband from the *Rex*. It is forty years since the French Line held the trophy with the *La Touraine* which soon lost it to the *Lucania*.

NORMANDIE

[By courtesy of Compagnie Générale Transatlantique]

1935, July 5th. Capt. Pugnet, her commander, lost his wife just as the ship was leaving Havre, after a long illness.

1935, Aug. Brought 1,800 French tourists to Britain and ship was open to inspection in Cowes Roads.

1935, Oct. It was announced that she would lay up for the winter.

1936. During her winter lay up she was fitted with four new propellers, and many alterations to her accommodation were made, and structural alterations were made to the hull. Her gross tonnage was increased.

1936, Apr. 28th. Left Havre on trials off Ushant. On her return it was announced that the results were beyond expectations, vibration being practically unfelt. On her return to Havre she lost a propeller.

1936, May 5th. Left Havre on her first voyage of the season.

1936, June 1st. Arrived at Havre and her average speeds for the trip were: 27th May, 28·31 knots; 28th May, 27 knots; 29th May, 29·43 knots; 30th May, 28·13 knots; 1st June, 29 knots. The average for the whole voyage being 28·31 knots.

1936, July. Captain Pugnet, her commander, retired and was replaced by Captain Pierre Thoreux. Born in Brittany in 1890, he won the Croix de Guerre during the war, when serving as Lieutenant in the armoured cruiser *Kleber*, which was sunk. He has commanded all the great ships of the French Line, including the *Paris* and *Ile de France*. He was formerly second commander to Captain Pugnet.

Her owners report that she made a profit of at least 15,000,000 francs during her first season (£200,000).

No. 2. QUEEN MARY. 1935

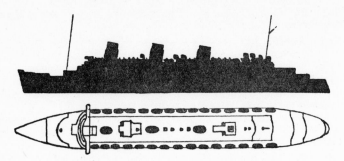

OWNERS:	Cunard White Star, Ltd.
SERVICE:	Southampton–New York.
NAT. & PORT:	British. Liverpool.
BUILDERS:	Messrs. John Brown & Co., Ltd., Clydebank, 1935.
TONNAGE:	80,773 tons gross.
DIMENSIONS:	1018 ft. lg. o.a. x 120 ft. o.a. width. 8 pass. decks.
ENGINES:	4 sets of Steam turbines, normal s.h.p. 180,000, capable of developing 200,000 s.h.p. Quad. screw. Normal speed 30 knots.
BOILERS:	24 water tube boilers in four separate boiler rooms, stm. pr. 400 lbs., 700 lbs. super heat. Three large cylindrical boilers in separate boiler room for auxiliary engine and hotel service, stm. pr. 250 lbs. First ship to have 2 separate boiler installations working at different pressures and with this division of service.
EL. LT. & PWR.:	2 complete power stations are provided, 1 forward containing 3 turbo-generators each rated at 1,300 k.w. at 220 volts, working of auxiliary boiler plant at 250 stm. pr. 4 turbo-generators in aft power station each 1,300 k.w. at 220 volts with stm. pr. at 400 lbs. supplied by main boilers. 2 emergency petrol-paraffin engine-generators are installed on upper deck, each 75 k.w. capacity.
PAINTWORK:	Hull black, red boot-topping, upper works white, funnels red with black tops and 3 black rings.
COMPLEMENT:	2,139 passengers in cabin, tourist and third classes, 1,100 officers and crew.

The stupendous majesty of this great vessel is tempered by her exquisite and graceful lines. This great ship contains all the palatial splendour combined with the home-like comfort of its smaller public rooms that the modern architect, artist, furnisher and decorator can give. She is truly a national ship and the great resources of the whole Empire with the skill of Britain's master craftsmen have made her the wonder of the age. A volume could be written about her wonders, but still first and foremost she is a ship which has a degree of seaworthiness, reliability and safety that never before has been reached by any vessel sailing the seven seas. As a ship she is superb, as an engineering job a marvel and as a floating hotel she has reached a pinnacle of perfection. The most magnificent ship that has ever worn the proud ensign of the British nation, she embodies the soul and pride of a nation of seafarers and master shipbuilders. The last of a long line of marvellous ships embodying the traditions of two great ship-owning companies, the senior of which has had almost a century of unbroken record making effort and enterprise on the Atlantic Ocean, a record unapproach-able by any similar organisation in the world. The tourist class accommodation is as spacious and beautiful as the first class of many other older vessels and the third class are catered for with such a high degree of comfort and roominess that has never before been attempted. Hot and cold water, dainty curtains and colourful carpets, dressing table and electric fan in every state room. Her magnificent restaurant, 160 ft. long by 118 ft. wide and 30 ft. high seats over 800 diners with ample space, and is large enough to comfortably accommodate a vessel of the size of the famous first Cunarder *Britannia*, with plenty of room to spare. One promenade deck is 750 ft. long—twice the length of the façade of Buckingham Palace. Her beautiful rooms would take pages to describe and include no less than three rooms in which dancing can be indulged in, two separate swimming pools, Winter Gardens, lounges, smoking rooms, libraries, gymnasiums, shops, writing rooms, and her spacious terraced decks both fore and aft with the great sun deck offer plenty of space for open air exercise, the total space for sports is approximately two acres.

A complete air conditioning plant is installed to regulate the temperature and the humidity of the fresh air supply to the principal rooms, a Grimell fire sprinkler system covers the whole of the passenger accommodation. There are twenty-four motor engined lifeboats, each with accommodation for 168 persons as well as numerous life saving rafts.

10,000,000 rivets have been used in her construction, which if placed end to end would stretch a distance of over 270 miles. There are more than 2,000 port holes and windows, the area of the glass being more than 2,500 square feet, the total weight of the stern frame and brackets is with the rudder nearly 600 tons, the rudder is the largest ever made and weighs over 140 tons. The lounge would comfortably hold nine double-decked omnibuses.

1930, Dec. The Chairman of the Cunard Line announced that the contract had been signed for her construction.

1931, Dec. 10th. Construction suspended owing to economic reasons.

1933. Negotiations entered into between the Government, Cunard Line and White Star Line.

1934, Jan. 1st. Agreement between the Cunard Line and White Star Line came into force, amalgamating the Atlantic interests of the two famous lines, and in May, 1934, the new Company, Cunard White Star Limited was registered, and construction was resumed with Government assistance.

1934, Sept. 26th. Launched in presence of His Majesty King George and Her Majesty the Queen, Her Majesty graciously performing the naming ceremony. The first British liner to have been launched in the presence of a reigning King and Queen and the first to be named after a reigning Queen. Launching weight given as 40,000 tons—a world's record. It was announced that she would leave the Clyde for speed and reliability trials, to take place in the Atlantic off the north-west coast of Ireland, in March, 1936.

1935, Nov. The Directors of Cunard White Star, Ltd., announced that they had appointed Captain Sir Edgar Britten, Commander of the *Berengaria* and Commodore of the Fleet, to be her first Commander.

1935, Dec. It was announced that she had been classed as a Cabin ship by the North Atlantic Conference.

1936, Mar. 26th. She left the Clyde for Southampton for dry docking preparatory to her speed trials.

1936, Mar. 27th. Arrived at Southampton, and was successfully dry docked. She remained in the dry dock until the 31st.

1936, Apr. 15th. Left Southampton for her trials with 1,000 people on board.

1936, Apr. 19th. Ran her speed trials off the Isle of Arran, no official figures

QUEEN MARY

were issued, but her builders and the Cunard White Star Line announced their entire satisfaction. An official estimate of her maximum speed was given as 32·84 knots.

1936, Apr. 20th.   Arrived back at Southampton and was berthed at Ocean Dock. She was insured for £4,800,000, of which £3,000,000 was placed in the open market and the remaining £1,800,000 was taken up by the British Government.

1936, May 6th.   Captain B. H. Davies, Staff Captain of the *Aquitania*, appointed Staff Captain.

1936, May 14th.   Left Southampton for a day's cruise with a large party of distinguished guests on board.

1936, May 16th.   A large party of Members of the Houses of Parliament made a tour of inspection of the vessel, and took luncheon on board.

1936, May 25th.   H.M. the King, Queen Mary, the Duke and Duchess of York, the Duke and Duchess of Kent, the Duchess of Gloucester, and Princess Elizabeth visited the vessel and inspected her.

1936, May 27th.   Left Southampton at 4.30 p.m., on her maiden voyage to New York, she had a great send off, thousands of people lined the quays to give her God-speed.

1936, June 1st.   Arrived at New York. She passed the Ambrose Light-vessel at 2-03 p.m., B.S.T., having made the passage from Cherbourg Break-water at an average speed of 29·133 knots, total time taken 4 days 12 hrs. 24 mins. She had a remarkable welcome and her arrival was cheered by hundreds of thousands of spectators.

1936, June 5th.   She left New York on her first homeward voyage at 3.56 p.m., B.S.T.

1936, June 10th.   Arrived at Southampton at 3.30 p.m., her time from Ambrose Light-vessel to Cherbourg being 4 days 15 hrs. 15 mins., the average speed being 28·74 knots.

1936, Aug. 25th.   She made the fastest westward crossing of the Atlantic, thus winning the Blue Riband of the Atlantic back to Britain after seven years, her average speed being 30·01 knots.   Time 4 days 7 hrs. and 12 mins.

1936, Aug. 31st.   She arrived back at Southampton at 12.40 p.m., and was given a great reception, Captain Edgar Britten being given a civic welcome.

Shoals of congratulatory messages were received and Sir Percy Bates, Chairman of the Cunard White Star Line, telegraphed his congratulations to Sir Edgar Britten, Chief Engineer Roberts and the crew on the result of her return voyage at the record speed of 30·63 knots.   Time 3 days 23 hrs. 57 mins. The first time a crossing has been made under the four days, *Normandie's* best eastward crossing was at an average speed of 30·31 knots.   Time 4 days 3 hrs. 28 mins.

1936, Sept. 3rd.   The fellow townsmen of Chief Engineer Roberts of Llandudno, North Wales, made him a presentation.

The Liverpool and London underwriters on behalf of the British Marine Insurance Companies presented to Sir Percy Bates a silver rose bowl for the *Queen Mary*.

The Rotarians of the Greater London District presented the ship with a beautiful polished brass bell mounted on a wooden plinth.

The Junior second officer of the ship is Mr. E. J. R. Pollitt, who was presented with the Board of Trade Silver medal by the late King George V, for his conspicuous gallantry in the rescue of the crew of the *Ulsworth*, on Dec. 14th, 1935, when serving as second officer in the *Ascania*. He was also awarded Lloyd's medal for saving life at sea.

Sir Percy Bates announced that the *Queen Mary's* sister ship would be in service by the spring of 1940. She was to be built by the same firm, Messrs. John Brown & Co., Ltd.

The Cunard White Star Line announced that they will not accept the " Hales Trophy " which marks the possession of the Blue Riband of the Atlantic, which is now held by the French Line. The Directors consider that a trophy set up for international competition introduces an undesirable element into the operation of big ships.

No. 3. MAJESTIC. 1914

(Ex Bismark)

OWNERS:	Cunard White Star, Ltd.
SERVICE:	Southampton–New York.
NAT. & PORT:	British. Liverpool.
BUILDERS:	Herrn Blohm & Voss Ges., Hamburg, 1914.
TONNAGE:	56,551 tons gross register.
DIMENSIONS:	956 ft. long o.a., 916 ft. lg. b.p. x 100 ft. beam. x 57 ft. depth. 8 decks.
ENGINES:	8 Parsons type steam turbines, 80,000 s.h.p. 4 screws. Normal speed 24 knots.
BOILERS:	46 S.E. boilers, stm. pr. 240 lbs., covering an area of 5 acres.
PAINTWORK:	Hull black with gold line, boot-topping red, upper works white, funnels buff with black tops.
COMPLEMENT:	4,000 passengers in 1st, 2nd and 3rd classes, and officers and crew of 1,093.

This great and splendid ship, the largest ship to be launched before the war, and the largest ship in commission prior to the *Normandie* and *Queen Mary*, is known as " Queen of the Western Ocean," and amongst sailormen as " Magic Stick." She is a beautifully equipped ship and noted for her spacious accommodation. Her funnels are 180 ft. high from the fire bars of her furnaces. When taken over by her new owners she was equipped with all the latest instruments and improvements for safety and navigation, being also the first liner to be equipped for " Talkies." Flagship of the fleet until the advent of *Queen Mary*. Her size is equal to that of the 132 ships which formed the Spanish Armada. Has library capacity of 4,000 volumes.

1913. Laid down at Hamburg for the Hamburg-Amerika Line.

1914. Launched, largest liner in the world to date. Work on her held up during war.

1919. Ceded to Great Britain by treaty of Versailles.

1920. Completed and handed over to British Shipping Controller. Sold by him to White Star Line, Oceanic Steam Navigation Co., Ltd., of Liverpool.

1923. Received complete overhaul, and furnaces converted to oil burning. In September, after going back into service she made a record crossing (for her) of the Atlantic at an average speed of 24·76 knots.

1931, Dec. Captain Trant, R.N.R., appointed commander, from *Olympic*.

1932. Captain Trant was appointed Commodore of White Star Fleet.

1934. Taken over with Atlantic fleets of the White Star and Cunard Lines by the new Company, Cunard White Star Ltd.

1934. Sept. On voyage she met huge Atlantic wave which poured tons of water into her, Captain Trant was injured and Staff Captain took over command. On arrival at Southampton, Captain Irving, R.N.R., of the *Berengaria*, was appointed in command during indisposition of Commodore Trant.

1934, Sept. She went aground off Calshot in the Isle of Wight, she was able to get off under her own power and was undamaged.

1935. Captain Robert B. Irving, R.D., R.N.R., was appointed Commander permanently. He is one of the most well known and popular Captains on the

MAJESTIC

Atlantic; in 1931 he relinquished command of the *Franconia* to take command of the *Aquitania* and in the same year he was appointed R.N.R. A.D.C. to H.M. the King, having been promoted to Captain in the Reserve in 1925. He received the Order of the British Empire for his splendid work during the War. Later he was appointed Commander of the *Berengaria*.

1936, May 5th. After being withdrawn from service, she was offered for sale for scrapping.

1936, May 15th. The sale to Messrs. Thos. Ward, Ltd., was announced, price paid said to be £115,000. She is the largest ship ever to be sold for scrapping.

It was, however, later announced that this fine ship had been purchased by the British Admiralty, to be used as a training ship for apprentice seamen. She will be stationed at Rosyth after extensive alterations.

No. 4. BERENGARIA. 1912

(Ex Imperator)

OWNERS:	Cunard White Star Line, Ltd.
SERVICE:	Southampton–Cherbourg–New York.
NAT. & PORT:	British. Liverpool.
BUILDERS:	Vulkan Werkes, Akt. Ges., Hamburg, 1912.
TONNAGE:	52,022 tons gross register.
DIMENSIONS:	919 ft. long o.a., 882 ft. 9 in. lg. b.p. x 98·5 ft. breadth x 63 ft. depth. Draught 35 ft. 6 in. 8 decks.
ENGINES:	4 sets of Curtis-A.E.G.-Vulkan steam turbines, 62,000 s.h.p. ahead and 35,000 s.h.p. astern. 4 screws. Normal speed 23 knots.
BOILERS:	46 water tube boilers in 4 boiler rooms each about 70 ft. long.
PAINTWORK:	Hull black, boot-topping red, with white band on waterline, upper works white, funnels red with black top and 3 narrow black bands.
EL. LT. & PWR.:	5 turbine-generators. 10,000 lights.
COMPLEMENT:	2,500 passengers, 950 officers and crew.

The first of the three giants built for the Hamburg–Amerika Line, and the first large German liner to be fitted with steam turbines. A beautiful ship with somewhat finer lines than the *Majestic* and *Leviathan*. She has very luxurious and spacious accommodation and is a great favourite with Atlantic travellers. Has a large swimming bath, magnificent ballroom, up-to-date gymnasium, beautiful palm court, garden verandah café, Turkish and sun baths, and regal suites of rooms. One of the immense rotors of her turbines containing 50,000 blades, weighs 135 tons, the whole of the turbines contain some 760,000 blades.

1912, May 23rd. Launched by ex-Kaiser.

1913. Maiden voyage, from Hamburg to New York.

1914, Aug. 1st. Scheduled to leave Hamburg for New York, but sailing was cancelled, and she never went to sea again under her original flag.

1919. Ceded to Great Britain under treaty of Versailles. Sold by British Shipping Controller to Cunard Line and name changed.

1920, Feb. 2nd. Left Liverpool on her first voyage under Cunard flag.

1922. Completely re-fitted and her furnaces converted for oil burning.
1930. Captain Edgar Britten, R.D., R.N.R., appointed her Commander.

1933, Nov. 15th. Received S O S from British s.s. *Saxilby*, sinking in Atlantic, with crew of 27 on board. *Berengaria* altered her course and on reaching position given in last radio message no trace of the *Saxilby* or any boats or survivors was found.

1934. She received an extensive overhaul.

1934. Her Commander, Captain Sir Edgar Britten, R.D., R.N.R., was appointed Commodore of the new Cunard White Star Fleet.

1934. Encountered a hundred mile an hour gale in Atlantic, making her a day late. She made a record turn round at Southampton by leaving for New York after only 15¾ hours in port, an army of carpenters worked all night repairing the damage done during the voyage from New York in the terrific gale.

1935, Sept. 11th. Left Southampton for New York after another record-making turn round, being on this occasion only 13¼ hours in port; during this short stay more than a thousand passengers and their baggage were dealt with and over 4,000 bags of mail handled. 7,000 tons of oil fuel were pumped into her bunkers, a million gallons of fresh water pumped into her tanks, and 30 tons of ships' stores were taken on board besides some express cargo.

1936, Oct. 20th. While undergoing an overhaul at Southampton, several cabins caught fire. Her next sailing was Nov. 18th, 1936, when she relieved the *Aquitania* on the New York service with the *Queen Mary*. She is the last of the three great Hamburg-Amerika liners to remain in service.

BERENGARIA

By courtesy of the Cunard White Star Line

No. 5. BREMEN. 1928

Silhouette before funnels were raised.

OWNERS:	Norddeutscher Lloyd Co.
SERVICE:	Bremen–Southampton–New York.
NAT. & PORT:	German. Bremen.
BUILDERS:	German Shipbuilding & Engineering Co., Weser Yard, Bremen, 1928.
TONNAGE:	51,731 tons gross.
DIMENSIONS:	938 ft. lg. o.a., 899 ft. lg. b.p. x 102 ft. beam. x 54 ft. depth. 7 decks.
ENGINES:	4 sets of steam turbines, single red. gearing, 1800-180 r.p.m., 125,000 s.h.p. at normal speed. Quad. screw. Normal speed 27·5 knots.
BOILERS:	20 water tube, stm. pr. 330 lbs., 700 deg. F. super heat. Oil fuel. Consumption 830 tons per day at normal speed.
PAINTWORK:	Hull black, boot-topping red, with white band on water line. Upper works white, funnels buff.
COMPLEMENT:	600 1st, 500 2nd, 300 tourist, 1,100 3rd class, crew of 950.
REMARKS:	22 large steel lifeboats, and 4 smaller and 2 other boats; large boats are motor driven and can do 6 knots with 145 persons on board, lifeboats mounted on Wellin-Maclachlan patent davits. At one time had an aeroplane catapult between her funnels. Fitted with "Oertz" rudder.

A magnificent ship of modern design, and beautiful lines, fitted with bulbous bow. The original *Bremen* of the N.D.L. was their first Transatlantic liner built in 1858 and was 334 ft. lg. x 42 ft. beam, her first passage to New York took 14 days in bad weather, and the return trip in 12 days 5 hours.

1926, Dec. Contract was placed with builders. 1927, May. Laid down.

1928, June 16th. Launched in the presence of Prince von Hindenburg. Launching weight, 32,000 tons.

1929. On steam trials made 28·5 knots developing 140,000 s.h.p.

1929, July 16th. Left Bremen for New York on her maiden trip, on July 22nd on her arrival at New York she was presented with a fine bronze plaque which has been fixed in a prominent position on board. The inscription reads:— " *Bremen*, Queen of the Seas, 27th July, 1929, presented to the Norddeutscher Lloyd Line by the Association of German Societies in the City of New York." She broke both east and westbound records held by *Mauretania* since 1907, her average speed being eastbound 27·83 knots, and 27·9 knots westbound.

1931. Dr. Gertrude Ferber was appointed Captain's secretary and ship's hostess, at her own suggestion, first ship to have such an official on board. Her duties include deputising for the Captain in social affairs and advising passengers.

1932, Dec. Made new westbound record crossing by arriving at New York from Cherbourg in 4 days 15 hrs. 56 mins.

1933, June. Crossed from New York to Cherbourg at average speed of 28·51 knots.

1934, Nov. Made her 100th crossing and broke her own record by passing Ambrose light in 4 days 15 hrs. 27 mins. from Cherbourg.

BREMEN
(Before funnels were raised.)

[By courtesy of the Norddeutscher Lloyd Line

No. 6. REX. 1932

OWNERS:	Italian United Fleet. Italia Line.
SERVICE:	Genoa–New York.
NAT. & PORT:	Italian. Genoa.
BUILDERS:	Soc. Anon. Ansaldo, Sestri, Ponente, Italy, 1932.
TONNAGE:	51,062 tons gross. 30,623 tons nett.
DIMENSIONS:	879·9 ft. lg. o.a., 833·8 ft. lg. b.p. x 97 ft. beam. x depth 47ft. 3in. 7 decks.
ENGINES:	12 steam turbines, sin. red. geared to 4 shafts. 120,000 s.h.p. Quad screw. Normal speed 28 knots.
BOILERS:	14 water tube, fitted with super heaters 384 lbs. stm. pr. 735 deg. s.h. The turbines and boilers are grouped in separate water tight compartments so as to ensure that at least 2 of the turbines with boiler power will be in operation in the event of trouble. Oil fuel.
EL. LT. & PWR.:	Savoia-M.A.N. Diesel engine generators totalling 5,300 k.w.
PAINTWORK:	Black hull, boot-topping red with white dividing line, white upper works, funnels white with narrow green band and red top.
COMPLEMENT:	378 1st, 378 2nd, 410 tourist, 866 3rd class passengers.
REMARKS:	24 lifeboats, 22 of which are motor driven, and 4 are fitted with wireless. Vessel is divided into 15 watertight compartments.

The Royal majesty of her name corresponds to the stateliness of the vessel. The public rooms of incomparable luxury include ballroom, music rooms, lounge, card rooms, writing rooms, chapel, Winter Garden, verandahs, two swimming pools with lido and gymnasium. The ballroom is an exceptionally beautiful room, has a floor area of 7,200 sq. ft. and is one of the largest rooms afloat.

1932, Sept. Steam trials, averaged 28·9 knots on 9 hours, trial developed 140,000 s.h.p.

1932, Sept. 27th. Left Genoa on her maiden voyage, unfortunately had turbine trouble when off Gibraltar and put in for repairs.

1933, Aug. Did record voyage, Gibraltar to Ambrose light, N.Y. 4 days 13 hrs. 38 mins., average speed of 28·92 knots, winning the Atlantic Blue Riband from the *Bremen*.

1935, Aug. The Trophy was presented to the Italia Line.

REX

[*By courtesy of "Italia" Line*

No. 7. EUROPA. 1930

OWNERS:	North German Lloyd Co.
SERVICE:	Bremen–Southampton–New York.
NAT. & PORT:	German. Bremen.
BUILDERS:	Blom & Voss, Hamburg, 1930.
TONNAGE:	49,746 tons gross.
DIMENSIONS:	890·2 ft. lg. b.p. x 102·1 ft. beam. x 48 ft. depth. 5 decks.
ENGINES:	4 sets of steam turbines (12) geared to 4 scr. shts. 125,000 s.h.p. at normal speed. Quad. screw. Normal speed 27·5 kts.
BOILERS:	20 water tube, 330 lbs. per sq. in. at 700 deg. super heat. Oil fuel.
PASS. ACCOM.:	600 1st, 500 2nd, 300 tourist, 1,100 3rd class.
PAINTWORK:	Hull black, boot-topping red, white band on water line, upper works white, funnels buff.

Sister ship to *Bremen*, but slightly shorter. At one time carried an aeroplane which was launched from the ship when 600 miles out in either direction, and so delivered mails in Europe and America one day earlier. The aeroplane was launched by means of a special catapult.

Her funnels are not stream-lined like those of the *Bremen*, but are of normal elliptical section and her rudder is an ordinary balanced single plate type. Passenger accommodation is very luxurious and spacious, a notable feature being the street of shops, and a lofty Winter Garden, semi-circular in shape. 180 rooms have private baths and a further 100 with private shower baths.

Like her sister ship she has a Captain's secretary and ship's hostess, Fraulein Elli Dackau, being the first holder of the post.

1929, Mar. 26th. On fire during fitting-out at builders' yard.

1930, Mar. 25th. Maiden voyage. Record passage Cherbourg to New York in 4 days 17 hrs. 6 mins. 27·91 knots average speed.

Held Atlantic Blue Riband until beaten by her sister ship *Bremen*.

1933, Sept. By using her seaplane catapult she delivered her New York mails in London in the record time of four days.

1932, Dec. Capt. Nicolaus Johnsen died in New York after operation at sea.

1935, Feb. 27th. Received S O S from the Glasgow steamer *Blairgowrie* in distress in Atlantic, went to her assistance but found no trace of ship or life-boats.

EUROPA

No. 8. LEVIATHAN. 1914

(Ex Vaterland)

OWNERS:	United States Lines.
SERVICE:	New York–Southampton–Bremen.
NAT. & PORT:	United States. New York.
BUILDERS:	Blom & Voss, Hamburg. Built for Hamburg–Amerika Line, 1914
TONNAGE:	48,943 tons gross.
DIMENSIONS:	950·7 ft. lg. o.a. x 100 ft. beam. x 58 ft. depth. Draught 37 ft. 907 ft. lg. b.p. 6 decks.
ENGINES:	4 sets of steam turbines, 80,000 s.h.p. at normal speed. Quad screw. Normal speed 24 kts.
BOILERS:	46 Single ended, 235 lbs. per sq. in. steam pressure. Oil fuel.
PAINTWORK:	Hull black, upper works white, funnels red with white band and blue tops.

Her palatial and picturesque public rooms are models of artistic decoration, the dining saloon and Winter Garden being of special note.

Was largest ship afloat to date. Second of the giant Hamburg–Amerika liners.

1914, Aug. On her second trip was interned in New York.

1917. Taken over by United States Government and used as troopship, carried as many as 10,000 troops in one trip. Known to the U.S. troops as the " Levi Nathan."

1919. Was re-fitted and gross tonnage increased to 59,977 tons, making her the largest ship afloat although 7 ft. shorter than the *Majestic*. Her elaborate German decorations were replaced by more modern schemes, coalfired boilers converted to oil burning, making a reduction in her engine room staff of 225 men. Passenger accommodation was then 978 1st, 548 2nd, and 2,117 3rd class.

1923. Went into service with 1,150 officers and crew. On trials did 1 hour run at 27·075 knots.

1930 to 1933. Commanded by Capt. Randall, Commodore of Line.

1931. Her gross tonnage was reduced to 48,943 tons. It was estimated that her increased tonnage had cost the owners over £100,000 in increased dry dock and harbour dues, etc.

1933, Dec. Laid up as unprofitable to run.

1934, June. Resumed service after reconditioning at a cost of £30,000, it being estimated that £12,000,000 had now been spent on her by her American owners since taking her over during the War.

1934, Sept. Withdrawn from service after five round trips which made a heavy loss.

1935, July. It was suggested to the American Government that she, along with *George Washington* and *America*, should be used as training depots for merchant marine officers and crews.

LEVIATHAN

No. 9. CONTE di SAVOIA. 1932

OWNERS: The Italian United Fleet, Italia Line.

SERVICE: Genoa–New York.

NAT. & PORT: Italian. Genoa.

BUILDERS: Cantieri Riuniti Dell Adriatico, Trieste, Italy, 1932.

TONNAGE: 48,502 tons gross, 25,948 tons nett.

DIMENSIONS: 860 ft. o.a., 814·6 ft. lg. b.p., 96 ft. beam. Depth 113 ft. from keel to top of bridge. 7 decks.

ENGINES: 4 sets of steam turbines sin. red. grd. to 4 shfts., 120,000 s.h.p. Oil fuel. Tank capacity of 7,000 tons. Quad. screw. Normal speed 28 kts.

BOILERS: 10 Yarrow water tube, 425 lbs. st. pr. at 730 deg. F. s.h.

EL. LT. & PWR.: 4 steam turbo-generators and 2 Diesel-generators, totalling 5,300 k.w. No. of lights aboard 18,000.

PAINTWORK: Hull black, boot-topping red with white dividing line, upper works white, funnels white with narrow green band and red tops.

COMPLEMENT: 378 1st, 378 2nd, 410 tourist, 860 3rd class passengers.

REMARKS: 26 lifeboats, 22 of which are motor driven, each accommodating 137 persons. Vessel is divided into 13 watertight compartments. Fitted with Brown Bros. patent hydraulic steering gear. Refrigerators by Hall, Ltd., of Dartford. Electric log equipment and Sperry gyroscope stabilisers making her " The ship that cannot roll." Similar ship to the *Rex* but not quite so large or so fast.

A great ship which in six and a half days unites Genoa and New York, offers in pleasant and harmonious surroundings every conceivable comfort of modern social life. The fine features of her build and engineering find a counterpart in her sumptuous fittings, the variety and size of her public rooms satisfies the most fastidious. The well designed lounge, large galleries which run from one end of the ship to the other, the stately " Colonna Hall," Winter Garden, open and enclosed swimming pools, and marble walled dining-room together with the round shaped Night Club, Bamboo Bar, offer her passengers a full range of exquisite refinements.

1932, Nov. Speed trials, attaining a speed of over 30 knots and an average of 28 knots.

1932, Nov. 30th. Left Genoa for New York on her maiden voyage, was unfortunately obliged to stop when 800 miles from New York owing to a broken exhaust valve belonging to a turbo-generator.

CONTE DI SAVOIA

No. 10. BRITANNIC. 1914

OWNERS:	White Star Line.
SERVICE:	Intended for Southampton–New York Service.
NAT. & PORT:	British. Liverpool.
BUILDERS:	Harland & Wolff, Ltd., Belfast, 1914.
TONNAGE:	48,158 tons gross.
DIMENSIONS:	900 ft. lg. o.a., 852 ft. lg. b.p. x 94 ft. beam. x 80 ft. depth. Draught 34 ft. 6 in.
ENGINES:	2 Quadruple expansion reciprocating engines, 4 cyls. each on outside shafts and low pressure turbine on centre shaft. 50,000 s.h.p. at normal speed. Triple screw. Normal speed 21 kts.
BOILERS:	29 boilers each weighing 105 tons.
PAINTWORK:	Hull black with gold line, boot-topping red, upper works white, funnels buff with black tops.

Cost £2,000,000 to build, largest British built liner prior to *Queen Mary*.

1914, Feb. Launched. Completed after outbreak of the Great War and immediately taken over by Admiralty. Commissioned as Hospital ship.

1916, Feb. 21st. Sunk by mines laid by submarine in Aegean Sea; twenty-one of crew and nine hospital staff killed.

BRITANNIC   *By courtesy of Cunard White Star Li*

No. 11. TITANIC. 1912

OWNERS:	White Star Line.
SERVICE:	Southampton–New York.
NAT. & PORT:	British. Liverpool.
BUILDERS:	Harland & Wolff, Ltd., Belfast, 1912.
TONNAGE:	46,500 tons gross.
DIMENSIONS:	882·9 ft. x 92·6 ft. beam x 64·3 ft. depth. 5 decks.
ENGINES:	2 Quad. exp. 4 cyl. recip. engs. on outside shafts and 1 low pressure turbine on centre shaft. 46,000 s.h.p. Triple screw. Normal speed 22½ kts.
BOILERS:	29 boilers, steam pressure 215 lbs.
COMPLEMENT:	Over 2,000 passengers and 853 officers and men.
PAINTWORK:	Hull black with gold line, boot-topping red, upper works white. Funnels buff with black tops.
REMARKS:	Launching weight 24,600 tons. Largest liner to date.

1912, Apr. 10th. Left Southampton on maiden voyage, with 1,308 passengers, 898 officers and crew, and 3,418 sacks of mail.

Apr. 14th. Informed from wireless from s.s. *Baltic* and s.s. *Caronia* that ice was about.

Apr. 15th. 2.20 a.m. She struck iceberg and sunk just before daybreak. The *Carpathia* answered wireless S O S (Capt. Rostron), and arrived on scene of sinking at daybreak, rescuing 711 persons who had left the ill-fated ship in boats and rafts; 1,595 passengers and crew had gone down with ship. The *Olympic* (sister ship), the *Baltic* and the *Virginian* also answered S O S, but were too far away to be of any assistance. The *Californian* was near to scene of the disaster but did not receive wireless call. Only one officer and four juniors who had charge of boats were saved out of over 50 officers and engineers who were on board. Captain Smith went down with his ship.

The full story of this disaster is graphically described in Commander Lightoller's book *Titanic and Other Ships*. Commander Lightoller being the only surviving senior officer.

No. 12. OLYMPIC. 1911

OWNERS: Cunard White Star Line.

SERVICE: Southampton–Cherbourg–New York.

NAT. & PORT: British. Liverpool.

BUILDERS: Harland & Wolff, Ltd., Belfast, 1911.

TONNAGE: 46,493 tons gross.

DIMENSIONS: 892 ft. lg. o.a., 852·5 ft. lg. b.p. x 92·5 beam x 59 ft. depth. Draught 34 ft. 6 in. 5 decks.

ENGINES: 2 Quad. exp. 4 cyl. recip. engs. on outside shafts and one low pressure turbine on centre shaft. 46,000 s.h.p. Triple screw. Normal speed 22½ knots.

BOILERS: 24 D.E. & 5 S.E. boilers, steam pr. 215 lbs. per sq. in.

PAINTWORK: Black hull, red boot-topping, gold band, white upper works. Funnels buff with black tops.

COMPLEMENT: 2,021 pass. in 1st class, tourist class and 3rd class. Crew: 853 officers and men.

REMARKS: Launching weight 24,600 tons; largest liner in world to date.

Her accommodation was noted for its spaciousness, and she was furnished and decorated in a richness combined with the best of good taste. To traverse the whole of her decks meant a walk of nine miles. Her huge funnels would take, if laid down, two railway trains abreast. Capt. Smith, first commander, left her to take *Titanic*.

1912. On maiden voyage was rammed and holed above waterline by H.M. Cruiser *Hawke*. Had a deck removed and structural alterations by builders.

1914. On war service.

1918, May 12th. When transporting U.S. troops rammed and sank German submarine U 103 during her 22nd voyage as troopship. Her commander, Capt. Bertram Hayes, who was afterwards knighted, was awarded the D.S.O. She was known to troops as " Old Reliable."

1921. Converted to oil fuel and re-fitted at cost of £500,000.

1929. Her Commander, Captain Walter Henry Parker, retired in December; he had formerly command of *Homeric*, and was very popular with Atlantic passengers. He died at Woking, Surrey, in November, 1935, aged 66, at the same time as his last ship was being dismantled.

1931. Capt. Binks appointed commander.

1932. Had a considerable refit, occupying three months, *Georgic* taking her sailings.

1934, May 16th. Rammed and sank the famous Nantucket Lightship off the U.S. Coast in a thick fog (Capt. J. W. Binks in command), U.S. Govt. claiming half a million dollars compensation. The crew of Lightship numbering seven were all drowned.

1934, Dec. Her Commander, Capt. Binks, retired after 45 years at sea.

1935, Mar. Withdrawn from service.

1935, July. Rumoured that Italian Government were negotiating for her.

1935, Aug. 20th. Opened for inspection by intending purchasers, largest vessel yet offered for sale for scrapping.

1935, Sept. 10th. It was announced that she had been bought by Sir John Jervis for £100,000 and re-sold by him to Messrs. Thomas Ward & Co., Ltd., for the same amount on the understanding that she was broken up at Jarrow.

1935, Oct. 11th. Left Southampton for Jarrow-on-Tyne, her last voyage.

OLYMPIC

[By courtesy of Cunard White Star Line

No. 13. AQUITANIA. 1914

OWNERS:	Cunard White Star Line, Ltd.
SERVICE:	Southampton–New York.
NAT. & PORT:	British. Liverpool.
BUILDERS:	John Brown, Ltd., Clydebank, 1914.
TONNAGE:	45,647 tons gross.
DIMENSIONS:	902 ft. lg. o.a., 869 ft. lg. b.p. x 97 ft. beam x 64 ft. 6 in. dep. Drt. 36 ft. 5 decks.
ENGINES:	4 sets of Parsons Steam turbines, 60,000 s.h.p. Quad. screw. Normal speed 23 knots.
BOILERS:	21 Scotch boilers, stm. pr. 195 lbs., 168 furnaces, oil fuel.
PAINTWORK:	Hull black with red boot-topping and white dividing line, upper works white, funnels red with 3 black rings and black top.
COMPLEMENT:	3,250 passengers and crew of 850.

The " ship beautiful " as she is often called, cost over £2,000,000, and being built without Government assistance she was designed for luxurious travel at moderate speed. She is said to have carried more passengers than any other Atlantic liner. A view of the great ship's artistically furnished public rooms justifies the claim that she is a ship beautiful. The Louis XVI dining-room, with its impressive height and skilful arrangement, produces an atmosphere resembling that of a fine old château rather than a room on shipboard. The grandeur of the Palladian Lounge on "A" deck, with its finely restrained decorations, was recently brightened by the introduction of fresh colourings. The ceiling is adorned by a fine old Dutch painting. There is a long gallery leading from the lounge to the smoking room with a wealth of interesting prints and polished woodwork. The smoking room is an adaption from Greenwich Hospital, the period being late Charles II, with solid oak panelling. There are also writing rooms, garden lounge, Egyptian swimming bath, gymnasium, cinema, promenade and sports decks. The re-frigerating plant has a capacity of 30 tons of ice every 24 hours. The machinery space occupies a length of 450 ft. There are no fewer than 150 auxiliary machines for ventilating, sanitation, cold storage, pumping, etc. Over 700 miles of electric cables, 10,000 electric lamps, and 1,500 electric bell pushes. Each propeller weighs 17½ tons.

1913, Apr. 21st. Launched by the Countess of Derby.

1914, May 30th. Commenced maiden voyage from Liverpool.

1914, Aug. Had completed her third round trip when she was requisitioned by the Admiralty and commissioned as armed cruiser, but being found too expensive to run she was paid off.

1915. Employed as a troopship and later as hospital ship.

1920. Was given an extensive re-fit and converted to oil burning at a cost of £400,000. With oil fuel her engine room staff was reduced by no less than 300 men, and a great saving in time in port was made possible.

1933. Was again re-fitted and rejuvenated, 1,000 men being employed in her for three months, talkie-cinema installed.

1934, Jan. 26th. Went aground at Calshot Spit, refloated after 2½ hours, with assistance of tugs, quite undamaged.

1934, June. Made record passage in 5 days 13 hours 40 mins. at an average speed of 23.92 knots.

1935, Apr. 11th. When returning to Southampton from a Mediterranean cruise she went aground off Southampton in a 60 mile an hour gale, and was refloated in about 26 hours with the assistance of 11 tugs. No damage.

She has been selected to operate the Southampton–New York service with the *Queen Mary*, and *Berengaria*.

AQUITANIA

No. 14. ILE DE FRANCE. 1926

OWNERS:	Compagnie Generale Transatlantique, the French Line.
SERVICE:	Havre–Southampton–New York.
NAT. & PORT:	French. Havre.
BUILDERS:	Ch. & Atel. de St Nazaire, St Nazaire, France, 1926.
TONNAGE:	43,450 tons gross.
DIMENSIONS:	763·7 ft. lg. x 92 ft. beam x 55·9 ft. depth.
ENGINES:	4 sets of steam turbines. 52,000 s.h.p. Quad. screw. Normal speed 23 kts.
BOILERS:	24 water tube boilers. stm. pr. 228 lbs. Oil fuel.
COMPLEMENT:	1,500 passengers. 700 crew.
PAINTWORK:	Hull black, boot-topping red, upper works white, funnels red with black tops.
REMARKS:	Largest French liner prior to *Normandie*. Record voyage speed at average of 23·5 kts.

One of the finest ships to be built during the last decade, the Island of France, as her name is translated, and is derived from the old name of the district which now contains Paris. She has been an internationally popular success with her thousands of square feet of deck space, newly decorated salons, suites and foyers, her famous boulevard of shops, and her exquisite decorations and paintings are an inspiration. The Grand Foyer, four decks high with soft beautiful woods on every side, gives a restful aristocratic atmosphere of France afloat. The glass enclosed coffee terrace, modernistic smoking room, Rodier silk at the many tall windows of the Salon de Thé, the grand salon with its forty lacquered columns suggest palaces and her dining saloon three decks high is considered one of the most appropriate smart dining-rooms afloat, the chapel, almost a tiny cathedral, is impressive with its dignified altar, rich carpets and carved seats. Writing rooms and library, the quiet haunt of the scholar and zealous correspondent, with woodwork of French walnut together with the gymnasium and garage for 60 cars indeed make her a floating Island of France.

ILE DE FRANCE

No. 15. EMPRESS OF BRITAIN. 1931

OWNERS:	The Canadian Pacific Rly. Company.
SERVICE:	Southampton–Canada and Cruising.
NAT. & PORT:	British. London.
BUILDERS:	Messrs. John Brown & Co., Ltd., Clydebank, 1931.
TONNAGE:	42,348 tons gross register.
DIMENSIONS:	758 ft. long o.a., 733·3 ft. lg. b.p. x 97·8 ft. beam x 56 ft. depth. Draught 32 ft. 5 decks.
ENGINES:	12 steam turbines sin. red. geared to 4 screw shafts. 60,000 s.h.p. at normal speed. 4 screws. Normal speed 24 knots.
BOILERS:	9 water tube, 425 lbs. pr. at 725 deg. super heat. Oil fuel.
PAINTWORK:	Hull and upper works white, with green boot-topping and blue line round hull, funnels buff.
COMPLEMENT:	423 1st, 260 tourist, 470 3rd class passengers, officers and crew 700.
REMARKS:	Largest British built liner since war, prior to *Queen Mary*. Largest and fastest liner to Canada. Largest liner to make round the world cruises.

The splendid public rooms of this beautiful ship bear names expressive of their dignity and use. Imperial in its elegance is the Empress room or Ball-room, decorated by Sir John Lavery, it is fitted with a complete stage and "Talkie" equipment. "The Salle Jacques Cartier" is the dining-room, opulent in its decorative scheme by Mr. Frank Brangwyn. Mayfair is the name given to the lounge, decorated by Mr. Charles Allom, it is equipped with a complete concert stage. Magnificent in length, the Mall stretches from Mayfair to the Empress room, a lovely gallery designed by Mr. P. A. Staynes. Eastern imagery, lacquer and porcelain inspire the design of the "Cathay" Lounge smoking-room by Mr. Edmund Dulac and the Olympian swimming pool of translucent terrazzo glass combine to make her a real wonder ship, the luxury and beauty of which have never been seen before on the Canadian service.

1930, June 11th. Launched by the Duke of Windsor when Prince of Wales.

1932. She crossed Atlantic 12 times in 12 weeks.

1933. On world cruise, during which she passed through the Suez and Panama canals, the largest ship to do so. She also crossed Atlantic 14 times in 14 weeks, steaming a distance of over 42,000 miles to do so. Made record trip, fastest time to Canada at average speed of 25·01 knots.

1934. Made another record trip improving her average speed to 25·08 knots.

1934, Nov. Made round trip from Southampton to Quebec and back in 11 days 4 hrs. and 47 mins., including 26 hrs. 2 mins. stay at Quebec.

1934, Nov. Her Commander, Captain R. G. Latta, Commodore of C.P.R. Fleet, who retired in July, 1933, reported to have been appointed General Superintendent of the Line. Captain Latta who was her first Commander has steamed over 300,000 miles in her, including three round the world cruises.

1935, June. Arrived at Southampton 36 hours late through fog in the St. Lawrence and collision with the Newcastle s.s. *Kafiristan* shortly after leaving Quebec, the latter ship caught fire.

1935, July. It was stated by Sir Edward W. Beatty, president of the Canadian Pacific Railroad Company, that it was the intention of the company to build a sister ship to her in the near future.

1935, Dec. Her first commander Captain Robert Gilmore Latta who relinquished command in 1934 to become Manager of the Canadian Pacific Steamships, Ltd., at Montreal, was appointed General Manager of the Line, in place of Captain James Gillies who retired from the position owing to ill-health.

EMPRESS OF BRITAIN

[By permission of "Syren and Shipping"

No. 16. L'ATLANTIQUE. 1930

OWNERS:	Compagnie de Navigation Sud Atlantique.
SERVICE:	France–South American ports.
NAT. & PORT:	French. Bordeaux.
BUILDERS:	Ch. & Atel. de St Nazaire, St Nazaire, France, 1930.
TONNAGE:	40,946 tons gross.
DIMENSIONS:	713 ft. lg. x 92 ft. beam x 57·7 ft. depth. 5 decks.
ENGINES:	12 steam turbines geared to two screw shafts. 61,000 s.h.p. Twin screw.
PAINTWORK:	Hull black with white line, upper works white, boot-topping red, funnels buff with black tops.
REMARKS:	Cost 400,000,000 francs (£3,200,000 at par) to build.

1930, April. Launched. Second largest French liner prior to *Normandie* and largest liner ever to be on South American service.

1933, Jan. 4th. When on voyage from Bordeaux to Le Havre for refit, was burned out in English Channel, burning red hot hull was adrift in channel for 36 hours, a French war vessel stood by her ready to sink her if she became a menace to shipping. Finally taken in tow by tugs and taken to Havre still burning. Her Commander, Capt. Schoofs, was not on board her at time, but boarded her during her tow to Havre.

A deal of litigation between the owners and insurance underwriters came before the French courts, the owners claiming in full as total loss and the underwriters claiming that she was repairable, it was stated that Messrs. Harland & Wolff, Ltd., of Belfast, had made a firm offer to refit her for £1,230,000. Total cost to underwriters for total loss being £2,687,000. The courts decided in favour of the owners. In Jan., 1935, she was still laying in the port of Cherbourg, at a cost of £100 per day, and the underwriters refused to accept ownership of her.

1935, Oct. 18th. Announcement of yet another appeal by the Insurance Companies to the Appeal Court at Bordeaux.

1936, Jan. The Appeal Court decided in favour of owners.

1936, Feb. 24th. The burnt-out liner was sold to Messrs. Douglas & Ramsey, Ltd., of Glasgow, for breaking up. Price paid said to be £57,000.

1936, Mar. 6th. She left Cherbourg in tow for the Clyde, after being in port for three years.

1936, Mar. 10th. Arrived in the Clyde on her last voyage, in tow of four Dutch tugs. She is to be broken up by Messrs. Smith & Co., at Port Glasgow.

L'ATLANTIQUE

No. 17. PARIS. 1917

OWNERS:	Compagnie Generale Transatlantique, the French Line.
SERVICE:	Havre–New York.
NAT. & PORT:	French. Havre.
BUILDERS:	Ch. & Atel de St Nazaire, St Nazaire, France, 1917.
TONNAGE:	34,569 tons gross.
DIMENSIONS:	735 ft. lg. x 83 ft. beam x 59 ft. depth. 5 decks.
ENGINES:	4 direct acting steam turbines (Parsons type). 45,000 s.h.p. at normal speed. Quad. screws. Normal speed 22 knots.
BOILERS:	15 water tube boilers.
PAINTWORK:	Black hull, red boot-topping, white upper works, red funnels with black tops.
COMPLEMENT:	340 1st, 163 tourist, 409 3rd class passengers.
REMARKS:	Largest French Liner before *Ile de France*.

Her luxurious accommodation is aristrocatic and restrained, and has the allure of the old world combined with the efficiency of the new. Her dining saloon is noteworthy.

1913. Laid down.

1914. Launched. Largest French liner to date. Construction held up during war.

1921. Completed and put in service.

1928. Severe damage by fire when in dock at Le Havre.

1935. June. Soon after leaving New York a stowaway found on board, said he chose the *Paris* because he preferred French cooking.

PARIS

No. 18. HOMERIC. 1914-20
(Ex Columbus)

OWNERS: Cunard White Star Line.

SERVICE: Southampton–Cherbourg–New York and Cruising.

NAT. & PORT: British. Liverpool.

BUILDERS: F. Schichau, Danzig, 1914–20.

TONNAGE: 34,351 tons gross.

DIMENSIONS: 775 ft. lg. o.a., 751 ft. lg. b.p. x 83 ft. beam. x 54 ft. depth. Draug 35 ft. 3½ in. 5 decks.

ENGINES: 2 Quadruple expansion 4 cyl. engines, 52,000 s.h.p. Twin screw Normal speed 20·5 knots.

BOILERS: 12 double ended cylindrical, stm. pr. 210 lbs.

PAINTWORK: Black hull with gold band, red boot-topping, white upper work funnels buff with black tops.

COMPLEMENT: 1,550 passengers and 625 officers and crew.

REMARKS: Has a wonderful open air " Lido " and swimming pool.

Largest Twin screw steamship built, and largest with reciprocating engine

Laid down as *Columbus* for North German Lloyd Co. Construction held u during war. Completed in 1920 and ceded under Peace treaty to Great Britain

1922. Sold to White Star Line, renamed.

Has had a very successful career and is very popular on both Atlantic an cruising services.

1924. She was converted to oil burning and had extensive alterations b Harland & Wolff, Ltd., Belfast.

1932-5. She was used practically exclusively for cruising.

1935, Sept. 26th. It was announced in Southampton that she would be r placed on cruise commencing on the 28th by the *Franconia*, and that sh would be laid up for the winter at an anchorage off the Isle of Wight. Sh berthed after a successful cruise on Sept. 25th.

It was rumoured that her late owners were negotiating to re-purchase her

1936, Feb. 12th. Was offered for sale.

1936, Feb. 27th. It was announced that she had been purchased by Thos W. Ward, Ltd., Sheffield, for breaking up. The price paid was given as abou £75,000.

HOMERIC

No. 19. ROMA. 1926

OWNERS:	The United Italian Fleet, Italia Line.
SERVICE:	Genoa–New York.
NAT. & PORT:	Italian. Genoa.
BUILDERS:	Soc. Ansaldo. Anon. Sestri, Ponente, Italy, 1926.
TONNAGE:	32,583 tons gross. 19,358 tons nett.
DIMENSIONS:	710 ft. lg. oa., 705·6 ft. lg. b.p. x 82·8 beam x 98 ft. from keel to bridge. 4 decks.
ENGINES:	8 steam turbines grd. to 4 shfts. 33,000 s.h.p. Quad. screw. Normal speed 19 knots.
BOILERS:	9 D.E. and 4 S.E. boilers 220 lbs. stm. pr. F.D. Oil fuel.
PAINTWORK:	Black hull, boot-topping red with white dividing line, upper work white, funnels white with narrow green band and red tops.
COMPLEMENT:	2,700 passengers and crew.

Sister ship to *Augustus* except for engines.

Has 13 watertight compartments, 36 lifeboats fitted with wireless. In addition to her nautical and technical equipment she offers luxury and comfort, making an inimitable example of the shipbuilders' and naval architects' art.

On the Atlantic she has acquired popularity with an international public. The public rooms have exquisite decorations and furnishings. There is a vestibule and in the great hall is an imposing statue of the Goddess Roma by the sculptor Angelo Zanelli, 4 beautiful galleries lead from the hall fore and aft, an interesting feature is that the saloon dining accommodation is on two levels, an upper and a lower saloon, library, writing, smoke rooms, and a swimming pool with lido are also provided, together with a well equipped gymnasium.

ROMA *[By courtesy of "Italia" Line.*

No. 20. COLUMBUS. 1922

OWNERS:	North German Lloyd Line.
SERVICE:	Bremen–Southampton–New York and Cruising.
NAT. & PORT:	German. Bremen.
BUILDERS:	F. Schichau, Danzig, 1922.
TONNAGE:	32,565 tons gross.
DIMENSIONS:	749·6 ft. lg. oa., x 81 ft. beam x 49 ft. depth. 5 decks.
ENGINES:	2 Quad. exp. 4 cyl. engines. 22,000 s.h.p. Twin screw. Normal speed 23 knots.
BOILERS:	Oil fuel.
PAINTWORK:	Black hull, red boot-topping with white dividing line, white upper works, buff funnels.

The last big liner to be fitted with reciprocating engines, and Germany's first big post-war express liner. She is very similar to *Homeric* only she has shorter funnels. Is a beautifully proportioned vessel and has splendid accommodation with all modern luxuries and refinements. Her coming out proved to the world that Germany could again take her place amongst the owners of the super luxury liners, and she has proved a very successful vessel.

1924. Maiden voyage.

1928. Her reciprocating engines were removed and two single reduction geared turbines installed by Herrn Blohm & Voss at Hamburg, increasing her shaft horse power to 40,000, and her service speed to 23 knots.

COLUMBUS

No. 21. MAURETANIA. 1907

OWNERS:	Cunard White Star Line.
SERVICE:	Southampton–Cherbourg–New York.
NAT. & PORT:	British. Liverpool.
BUILDERS:	Messrs. Swan, Hunter & Wigham Richardson & Co., Ltd., New-castle, 1907.
TONNAGE:	30,696 tons gross.
DIMENSIONS:	787 ft. lg. o.a., 762 ft. lg. b.p. x 88 ft. beam x 57 ft. depth. Draught 36 ft. 7 decks.
ENGINES:	4 sets of Parsons steam turbines. 68,000 s.h.p. Quad screw. Normal speed 25 knots.
BOILERS:	23 D.E. & 2 S.E. Scotch boilers, 165 stm. pr. Weight of engines and boilers given as 9,400 tons.
PAINTWORK:	Hull black, red boot-topping with white dividing line, upper works white, funnels red with black tops and 3 black rings.
COMPLEMENT:	560 1st, 475 2nd, 1,300 3rd class. 1,896 officers and crew.

1906, Sept. 20th. Launched. Launching weight 16,800 tons.

1907, Nov. 3rd. Steam trials. Average speed 26·09 knots. Max. s.h.p. 78,275.

1907, Nov. 16th. Left Liverpool on maiden voyage. Average speed 22·21 knots.

1907, Nov. 30th. Return voyage. Average speed 23·69 knots.

1909, Mar. 3rd. Made westward crossing at 25·55 knots average speed.

1909, June 21st. Arrived at Queenstown after crossing from New York at an average speed of 25.88 knots.

1910, Sept. Broke all previous records by voyage at average speed of 26·06 knots.

1910, Dec. Crossed Atlantic twice including time in New York in 12 days and a few hours.

1914, Aug. Commissioned by Admiralty, shortly transferred to trooping and later as Hospital ship.

1916-7. Laid up at Greenock.

1917. Trooping with U.S. Troops.

1919. May. Left Government service.

1921. Refitted and converted to oil burning.

1928. Westward voyage at average speed of 25·63 knots, return voyage at average speed of 26·2 knots.

1929, June. Westward voyage at average speed of 26·85 knots, returned at average speed of 27·22 knots, did 106 mile run in English Channel from Eddy-stone Light to Cherbourg at average speed of 29·7 knots, then 22 years old and with original Parsons Turbines.

1933, July. When on cruise left Havanna for New York and travelled 603 miles at an average speed of 27·78 knots, 112 miles of which she did at an average of 32 knots.

1934, Oct. Withdrawn from service.

In one year she steamed 77,500 miles at an average speed of 25½ knots.

1935, June. Sold to Messrs. Bolchow Vaughan, shipbreakers, for scrapping.

1935, July 1st. Left Southampton for Rosyth, her last voyage. Her departure from Southampton being broadcast.

MAURETANIA

[By courtesy of Cunard White Star Line

No. 22. LUSITANIA. 1907

OWNERS:	Cunard Line.
SERVICE:	Liverpool–New York.
NAT. & PORT:	British. Liverpool.
BUILDERS:	Messrs. John Brown & Co., Ltd., Clydebank, 1907.
TONNAGE:	30,600 tons gross.
DIMENSIONS:	786·5 ft. o.a., lg. 762 ft. lg. b.p. x 88 ft. beam. x 57 ft. depth. Draught 36 ft. 7 decks.
ENGINES:	4 sets of Parsons Steam turbines. 68,000 s.h.p. Quad screw. Normal speed 25 knots.
BOILERS:	23 D.E. and 2 S.E. Scotch boilers, stm. pr. 195 lbs.
COMPLEMENT:	560 1st, 475 2nd, and 1,300 3rd class. Officers and crew approximately 1,896.
PAINTWORK:	Hull black, red boot-topping with white water-line, white upper works, funnels red with black tops and 3 black rings.

1906, Aug. Launched.

1907, July 29th. Steam trials, average speed 25·4 knots.

1907, Oct. Left Liverpool on maiden voyage.

1914, Aug. 5th. Left New York and made her slowest passage known (due to machinery trouble).

1914. Commissioned by Admiralty, but soon returned to owners.

1915, May 7th. On voyage from New York to Liverpool was torpedoed and sunk by German submarine off coast off South of Ireland. Two torpedoes struck her and she sank in 20 mins., Capt. Turner in command. 1,198 lives were lost, including many American passengers. This sinking of passenger ships without warning led to the United States entering into the War.

Capt. Turner was saved and died in Liverpool in 1933.

Her best passage was westward in 4 days 11 hrs. 42 min., eastward in 4 days 15 hrs. 52 mins. Average speed of 25·188 knots, best day's run 666 miles.

She never reached the speed of her sister ship *Mauretania*.

1935. An attempt to salve her gold cargo was begun by salvage ship *Orphir*, and in October it was announced that she had located the wreck. On Nov. 6th a memorial service was held on board the *Orphir* over the wreck. Thirty people, including some survivors, attended.

LUSITANIA

[By courtesy of Cunard White Star Line.

No. 23. AUGUSTUS. 1927

OWNERS:	The United Italian Fleet, Italia Line.
SERVICE:	Genoa–New York.
NAT. & PORT:	Italian. Genoa.
BUILDERS:	Ansaldo Soc. Anon. Sestri, Ponente, Italy, 1927.
TONNAGE:	30,400 tons gross.
DIMENSIONS:	710·9 ft. o.a., 665 ft. lg. b.p. x 83 ft. beam x 46·5 ft. depth. 4 decks.
ENGINES:	4 6-cyl. 2 st. d.a. oil engines. M.A.N. type. Cyls. 27-9/16 in. dia. 47¼ in. stroke. 28,000 s.h.p. at 125 r.p.m. Built by Cantiere Officine Savoia, Genoa. Installed in three watertight compartments. Quad. screw. Normal speed 19½ knots.
EL. LT. & PWR.:	3 Diesel-eng.-generators ea. 600 k.w. 5 Diesel-eng.-generators ea. 280 k.w.
PAINTWORK:	Black hull, boot-topping red with white dividing line, upper works white, funnels white, green band, red tops.
COMPLEMENT:	2,700 passengers and crew.
REMARKS:	Largest motor vessel in world.

Thirty-six lifeboats, two of which are fitted with motor engines, and wireless. The ship has thirteen watertight compartments, and is fitted with all the latest nautical appliances. All four classes of passengers are exceedingly well provided for. The spacious entrance hall with tourists' bureau and numerous shop windows, the palatial hall on the upper deck, with its early Renaissance decorations, dining saloon with decorations and furnishings in the style prevailing in Piedmont at the end of the eighteenth century, magnificent social hall with its damask, gilt decoration, and mirrors in the manner of the princely seventeenth century palaces at Palermo offer a continuous succession of beauty which arouses the keenest admiration. There are also a grill-room, in Japanese red lacquer, a library, commodious bar in the Sicilian style, and children's nursery. Spacious promenades and sport deck and swimming pool with lido, and a gymnasium. Dances and theatrical performances take place in the brilliantly lit social hall, together with an up to date "Talkie" outfit, showing the latest films. As on all "Italia" Line vessels a daily newspaper, *The Corriere del Mares*, is published.

1933. She carried out a big programme of cruises.

AUGUSTUS

[*By courtesy of " Italia " Line*]

No. 24. STATENDAM. 1929

OWNERS:	Holland-Amerika Line.
SERVICE:	Rotterdam–New York.
NAT. & PORT:	Dutch. Rotterdam.
BUILDERS:	Harland & Wolff, Ltd., Belfast, 1929. Completed at Wilton Shipyards at Rotterdam.
TONNAGE:	29,511 tons gross.
DIMENSIONS:	670·4 ft. lg. o.a. x 81·4 ft. beam. x 49 ft. depth. 6 decks. Overhanging top deck 84 ft. wide gives additional space. Normal speed 18 knots.
ENGINES:	6 steam turbines s.r. geared to 2 scr. shafts. 20,000 s.h.p. Twin screw.
BOILERS:	6 water tube, stm. pr. 430 lbs. F.D. 650 deg. super ht. Oil fuel.
PAINTWORK:	Hull black with yellow band boot-topping red, upper works white, funnels buff with one white band between two green.
COMPLEMENT:	1,670 passengers, crew of 600.

She is the largest Dutch liner, and is known as the "Queen of the Spotless Fleet," The liner's arrival at New York on her maiden voyage was a municipal event as it marked the 300th anniversary of the arrival of the first Dutch ships in America. It was Hendrick Hudson's *Half Moon* coming into the same waters that brought about the first settlement of what is now New York City. Third ship of name, the second was just nearing completion in Belfast when she was taken over by the Government and used as a troopship under the name of *Justicia* and was torpedoed and sunk just before the Armistice, 600 miles off the Irish coast. Has an imposing ballroom, library, smoking room, reception room, verandah café, and large promenade decks. Main dining saloon "where one dines like a king" is a spacious and beautiful room in Louis XVI style, has 64 windows to give it ample light and air. On the promenade deck is a great social hall, a room of real majestic dignity and one of the architectural and artistic glories of the ship, with high ceiling, crowned in the centre by a dome of multi-coloured glass, beautiful carved oak panels extend from floor to ceiling; adding a final note are three superb Gobelin tapestries, works of art that depict quaint old Dutch landscapes. The smoking room is in Old Dutch style with rich old oak panelling and furniture to match.

1929, Apr. 11th. Maiden voyage, Rotterdam to New York.

1929, Apr. 27th. Left New York on return voyage.

1936. The Line is building a new 30,000 ton ship to be named *Nieuw Amsterdam*.

STATENDAM

No. 25. CHAMPLAIN. 1932

OWNERS:	Compagnie Generale Transatlantique, the French Line.
SERVICE:	Havre–New York and Cruising.
NAT. & PORT:	French. Havre.
BUILDERS:	Ch. de Atel. de St Nazaire, St Nazaire, France, 1932.
TONNAGE:	28,910 tons gross.
DIMENSIONS:	641 ft. lg. x 85 ft. beam x 67 ft. depth. Draught 30 ft. 9 decks.
ENGINES:	6 steam turbines s.r. geared to two screw shafts, 24,000 s.h.p. Twin screw. Normal speed 20 knots.
BOILERS:	6 " Penhoet " water tube. stm. pr. 400 lbs. S.H. 662 deg.
PAINTWORK:	Hull black, red boot-topping, upper works white, funnel red with black top.
COMPLEMENT:	623 cabin, 308 tourist, 122 3rd class passengers. Crew of 559. Officers and men.

Flagship of the French Line's cabin fleet. Named after the famous French explorer "Samuel de Champlain," founder of Quebec. Notable for her spacious decks with flush hatch covers, lifeboats are on special platform between sun deck and promenade deck. The public rooms are decorated and furnished on the usual lavish scale of the French Line. The smoking room has wooden pillars carved with giant figures of kings, queens, jacks, hearts, diamonds, spades and clubs painted in brilliant red and black. The glass enclosed café terrace is very attractive and a semi-circular modern bar furnished in red leather is situated between the smoking room and café terrace. The dining saloon, two decks high, is 65 ft. long and has 94 tables mostly for 2 and 4 persons; it takes amidst all its modernity the delightful air of a Spanish patio, though the ceiling which gives the effect of being draped in gauzy parchment coloured curtains sifts a soft flattering light. Walls and staircases are of tawny marble, the other public rooms are all similarly beautiful. The tourist class passengers are particularly well catered for with comfort and efficiency.

1935, Aug. Sailings were delayed by strikes at Havre and Plymouth.

1935, Sept. Encountered the full force of the hurricane which ravaged Florida, making her five hours late in reaching Plymouth from New York.

CHAMPLAIN

No. 26. GEORGIC. 1932

OWNERS:	Cunard White Star Line.
SERVICE:	Liverpool–Southampton and New York.
NAT. & PORT:	British. Liverpool.
BUILDERS:	Harland & Wolff, Ltd., Belfast, 1932.
TONNAGE:	27,759 tons gross.
DIMENSIONS:	683·5 ft. lg. o.a., 680 ft. lg. b.p. x 82·4 ft. beam x 48 ft. dep. Draught 35 ft. 5 decks.
ENGINES:	2 Harland-B & W. 10 cyl. 4 st. d.a. oil engines. cyl. diam. 33 1/16 in., stroke 63 in., 110 r.p.m., 20,000 b.h.p. consumes 40 tons oil fuel per day. Twin screw. Normal speed 17·5 knots.
BOILERS:	4 main engine exhaust gas-fired boilers provide steam at sea for heating and cooking and 2 oil-fired boilers for port and sea use.
EL. LT. & PWR.	4-6 cyl. oil engine driven generators. There are nearly 200 electric motors on board ranging from 1 to 170 h.p.
PAINTWORK:	Hull black with gold line, boot-topping red, upper works white, funnels buff with black tops.
COMPLEMENT:	1,550 in cabin, tourist and third classes.
REMARKS:	Sister ship *Britannic*.

With her sister ship they are the largest British motor ships, and their engines are the largest single unit oil engines in the world. Were specially built cabin class ships for New York service. Externally the two ships show some differences, principally that the *Britannic* does not have a rounded bridge front. The most striking room is the cabin smoking room, where an endeavour to get away from the customary reproduction of a room ashore, an original note was introduced by panelling the room with horizontal flat section lacquer work in black and vermilion suggestive of the construction and quality of a modern steel vessel. The effect is both striking and pleasing. In addition to the many luxuries and amenities usually associated only with a first class liner, which were introduced by the *Britannic*, the *Georgic* has a spacious palm court where tea dances and other social functions are held. There are also de-luxe suites, a swimming pool, tennis courts, elevators, as well as an altar in the cabin lounge for religious services; children's play rooms in all classes. The staterooms of all classes have hot and cold running water, and many of the baths are fitted with hot and cold showers. The size of the vessel, the great saving in space taken by the propulsion machinery and the ingenious planning has given unusually ample space for public rooms and created a general air of spaciousness throughout the ship. She took two years to build, employing 2,000 men. 650 tons of rivets were put into her construction. Thirteen miles of piping were used in plumbing, and four miles of air ducts for ventilating purposes. 200 miles of electric wiring is installed, the electrical plant being large enough for a town of 30,000 population. Each propeller turns 140,000 times, and each piston travels a distance in the cylinders of 250 miles, each day.

1929, Nov. 29th. Keel laid. 1931, Nov. 12th. Launched.

1932, June 25th. Left Liverpool for New York on maiden voyage. Outward did an average speed of 16·46 knots, homeward did an average speed of 17·72 knots.

1933, April. Did westward voyage in 8 days 45 mins., at average speed of 18·43 knots. 1934, Dec. Her Commander, Captain F. Summers, retired.

1935, Jan. Cargo hold on fire in New York, delaying her sailing for a few hours, little damage done to ship.

1935, Apr. With *Britannic* was transferred to London—New York service being the two largest ships to use the Port of London.

GEORGIC

[By courtesy of the Cunard White Star Line

No. 27. CAP ARCONA. 1927

OWNERS:	Hamburg Sud Amerika Line.
SERVICE:	Hamburg–South American ports.
NAT. & PORT:	German. Hamburg.
BUILDERS:	Blohm & Voss, Hamburg, 1927.
TONNAGE:	27,560 tons gross. 15,011 tons nett.
DIMENSIONS:	643·5 ft. lg. o.a. x 84·6 ft. beam x 41 ft. depth.
ENGINES:	8 steam turbines s.r. geared to 2 sc. shafts. 24,000 s.h.p. Twin screw Normal speed 20 knots.
BOILERS:	8 water tube boilers. 300 lbs. stm. pr. Oil fuel.
PAINTWORK:	Hull black, boot-topping red, upper works white, funnels white with red tops.
COMPLEMENT:	575 1st class, 274 in 2nd, 520 in 3rd class.
REMARKS:	The Flagship of the H.S.A. Fleet and the largest ship on the South American run.

She is in appearance a larger *Cap Polonio* but of course is more modern and luxurious, being fitted with every possible device and appointment for the safety and comfort of passengers. Her public rooms include a spacious entrance hall, lounge, Winter Garden, smoking room, palatial dining saloon, large swimming pool, gymnasium, with sports deck for the more strenuous passengers. She quickly achieved popularity in South America, and she is the fourth German ship in size, and the largest German liner using the port of Hamburg.

On her boat deck there is a full sized lawn tennis court.

1927, May. Launched. Maiden voyage commenced Nov. 19th, 1927.

1932, Nov. Established a new record for South American run, Rio de Janeiro to Plymouth in under 11 days at an average speed of 20 knots.

CAP ARCONA

[By courtesy of the Hamburg Sud Amerika Line

No. 28. COLUMBIA. 1912

(Ex Belgenland, Ex Belgic.)

OWNERS:	Atlantic Transport Line of West Virginia.
SERVICE:	New York–Pacific Coast ports and Cruising.
NAT. & PORT:	United States. New York.
BUILDERS:	Messrs. Harland & Wolff, Ltd., Belfast, 1912.
TONNAGE:	27,132 tons gross.
DIMENSIONS:	696·5 ft. lg. o.a. x 78·9 ft. beam. x 49·6 ft. depth. Draught 36 ft. 4 decks.
ENGINES:	2 4 cyl. triple ex. reciprocating engines on outside shafts and one L.P. turbine on centre shaft, 11,230 s.h.p. Triple screw. Normal speed 17 knots.
BOILERS:	10 D.E. boilers, stm. pr. 215 lbs. per sq. in. F.D.
PAINTWORK:	White hull and upper works, boot-topping red, black funnels with white band.
COMPLEMENT:	2,100 passengers, 530 officers and crew.

1912. Laid down. First Atlantic liner with cruiser stern. Designed for 800 1st and 2,000 3rd class passengers, altered before launching to 660 1st, 350 2nd.

1914, March. Announced that her name would be *Belgenland*.

1914, Dec. 31st. Launched.

1917, June. She was hurriedly completed as a cargo vessel, re-named *Belgic*, and put in service by The International Mercantile Marine Co., Capt. R. D. Jones being in command.

1918. Converted to troopship in New York.

1919. New York—Hamburg service.

1921. Laid up at Liverpool until March, 1922, when she went to Belfast to be re-fitted and passenger accommodation completely re-arranged. Renamed *Belgenland* and put on Red Star Line service, Antwerp to New York.

1924. Diverted to London owing to strike in Antwerp and she was the largest vessel to use London Docks. Later went on round the world cruise.

1930. Cruising from New York.

1933–4. Cruising from London.

1934. Laid up in Tilbury Docks. Dec. transferred to U.S. Lines. Renamed *Columbia*, and flag and registry changed.

1935, Jan. 10th. Left Tilbury Docks for New York, Capt. Jenson, of the *President Roosevelt* in command. She looked well with her hull re-painted grey and white upper works.

1935. Employed on Panama Pacific Mail Line, New York to California, calling at San Diego with visitors to the Exposition.

1936, Feb. 12th. After being withdrawn from service, she was offered for sale.

1936, Apr. 3rd. It was announced that she had been sold to Messrs. Douglas & Ramsey, of Glasgow, for about £55,000, for breaking-up purposes.

1936, Apr. 11th. Captain James Gentle and a crew of 41 left Liverpool in the *Scythia* to bring over the *Columbia*; the engineers sailed in the *Manhattan*. *Columbia* is to be broken up by P. & W. Maclellan, Ltd., at Bo'ness in the Firth of Forth.

1936, May 4th. She arrived in the Firth of Forth, the end of her last voyage, where she was driven ashore under her own power for breaking-up.

COLUMBIA

No. 29. BRITANNIC. 1930

OWNERS:	Cunard White Star Line.
SERVICE:	Liverpool–Southampton–London and New York.
NAT. & PORT:	British. Liverpool.
BUILDERS:	Harland & Wolff, Ltd., Belfast, 1930.
TONNAGE:	26,493 tons gross.
DIMENSIONS:	683·5 ft. lg. o.a., 680 ft. lg. b.p. x 82·4 ft. beam x 48 ft. depth. decks. Draught 34 ft. 3 in.
ENGINES:	2 Harland-B & W. 10 cyl. 4 st. d.a. oil engines. cyl. diam. 33 1/16 in x 63 in. stroke. 110 r.p.m. 20,000 b.h.p. Twin Screw. Norma speed 17·5 knots.
BOILERS:	4 main exhaust gas-fired boilers for heating and cooking steam, an two oil-fired boilers for port and sea use.
EL. LT. & PWR.:	4 oil engine driven generators, each 500 k.w.
PAINTWORK:	Hull black with gold band, boot-topping red, upper works white funnels buff with black tops.
COMPLEMENT:	1,550 passengers in cabin, tourist and third classes.

Sister ship *Georgic*. The accommodation provided sets up a new standard for cabin class ships, noteworthy features being the beautiful swimming pool tennis courts, Louis XIV dining saloon, two decks high, the provision of lift for all classes and children's playrooms in the tourist and third classes. There is a picturesque card room in the French style of late Gothic at the forward end of the promenade deck. The lounge also on this deck is in the late eighteenth century English style made attractively modern with full length pier glasses and beautifully varied furnishings. Talkie apparatus is installed, and a resilient parquet floor provides for dancing. Leading from the lounge to the smoking room is a tastefully decorated long gallery which forms a pleasant promenade in inclement weather. The drawing room in old Colonial style with an Adam flavour is a beautiful retiring room. It is in here that the altar for religious services is found. The smoking room is a remarkable reconstruction of a Tudor room in an Elizabethan mansion and with modern luxury in the furniture is the ideal of masculine comfort, whilst outside is the verandah café—a pleasant resort in all weathers.

A 75 k.w. Diesel driven generator is installed above the margin line supplying light and power for essential services if, for any reason, the main sets are out of action. In the forward funnel is situated a smoke room for use of the engineers A double bottom extends the whole length of the ship, arranged for carrying fresh water, fuel oil and water ballast. The ship is divided into 13 watertight compartments. The size of the ship has given ample opportunities for spacious planning and the impression of restricted space so common on ships has been effectively eliminated. All auxiliary machinery is electrically driven, and over 7,000 lights are installed. The cooking, too, is electric.

BRITANNIC

BRITANNIC

1930, June 30th.   Left Liverpool on maiden voyage, Captain Trant in command. Average speed 17·04 knots.

1931.   Voyage average speed for year 17·58 knots, fastest voyage average 17·95 knots.

1930, Dec.–Apr., 1931.   Cruised 23,220 miles.

1933, June.   Did voyage at average speed of 19·5 knots with largest number of passengers carried by any Atlantic liner that year, 1,103.

1933, Dec.   Went aground on mud flats in Boston Harbour during dense fog, with 250 passengers on board, refloated in 12 hours undamaged.

1934, Dec. 13th.   Had slight fire on board at New York, in fan space.

1935, April.   With sister ship *Georgic* transferred to London–Southampton–New York service.

No. 30. EMPRESS OF JAPAN. 1929

OWNERS:	Canadian Pacific Rly.
SERVICE:	Vancouver–Japan and China.
NAT. & PORT:	British. London.
BUILDERS:	Fairfield Co., Ltd., Glasgow, 1929.
TONNAGE:	26,032 tons gross.
DIMENSIONS:	662 ft. lg. o.a., 644 ft. lg. b.p. x 83·8 ft. beam. x 44 ft. depth. Draught 30 ft. 6 in. 6 decks.
ENGINES:	6 steam turbines s.r. geared. 30,000 s.h.p. Twin screw. Normal speed 22 knots.
BOILERS:	6 water tube boilers. 425 lbs. stm. pr. 725 deg. s.h. F.D. Oil fuel.
PAINTWORK:	Hull white with blue band, upper works white, boot-topping green, funnels buff.
COMPLEMENT:	400 1st, 164 2nd, 100 3rd and 548 Asiatic passengers.

An improvement on the *Empress of Canada*, the largest and fastest liner on the Pacific Ocean. The superstructure consists of boat and promenade decks both over 300 ft. long topped by the navigating bridge which is 68 ft. above the load water line. Notable features are the Palm Court, long gallery, foyer, green and black swimming pool and a beautiful Cipollino marble decorated dining saloon and sun deck.

This delightful ship holds the Blue Riband of the Pacific and is the largest liner on regular service on the Pacific Ocean. She is generally recognised to be one of the most lovely ships in the world, and the Company are justified in their pride of her.

[*By courtesy of C.P.R. Co.*

EMPRESS OF JAPAN

No. 31. CONTE GRANDE. 1928

OWNERS:	The United Italian Fleet. Italia Line.
SERVICE:	Genoa–South America.
NAT. & PORT:	Italian. Genoa.
BUILDERS:	Stabilmento Tecnico, Trieste, 1928.
TONNAGE:	25,661 tons gross.
DIMENSIONS:	652·2 ft. lg. o.a. x 78 ft. beam. x 27 ft. depth. 4 decks.
ENGINES:	4 steam turbines d.r. geared to shafts. 30,000 s.h.p. Twin screw Normal speed 20 knots.
BOILERS:	7 D.E. & 2 S.E. boilers 200 lbs. stm. pr., F.D.
PAINTWORK:	Hull black, boot-topping red with white dividing line, upper work white, funnels white with green band and red tops.
COMPLEMENT:	578 1st, 256 2nd, 154 intermediate, 720 3rd class passengers. Officer and crew 532.

Sister ship, though slightly larger, to the *Conte Biancamano*. A fine pair o medium sized liners considered perfect in both construction and artistic tast of decorations. Vestibule is rich in tasteful decoration, ballroom in the styl of the Italian Renaissance Period, entrance hall containing fountains, statues precious carpets and fine furniture, splendid dining saloon with a gallery above smoking room with an adjoining bar, writing room in Elizabethan style children's nursery, verandah café, gymnasium and large enclosed swimmin, pool in the Japanese style, reveals the care which has been taken to make ; stay on board enjoyable. A number of suites with sitting room, stateroom an private bath are provided.

On trials did 22 knots.

1935, Aug. 8th. Arrived at Lisbon on way to Genoa with 800 passengers o board. Stated to have received message during voyage ordering her urgen return for mobilisation as troop transport.

CONTE GRANDE

[By courtesy of the "Italia" Line

No. 32. GEORGE WASHINGTON. 1908

OWNERS:	United States Lines.
SERVICE:	New York–Southampton–Bremen.
NAT. & PORT:	United States. New York.
BUILDERS:	Akt. Ges. Vulkan, Stettin, Germany, 1908.
TONNAGE:	25,570 tons gross. 15,379 tons nett.
DIMENSIONS:	699 ft. lg. o.a. x 78·2 ft. beam. x 50 ft. depth. 6 decks.
ENGINES:	2 Quad. exp. recip. engines 14,200 s.h.p. Twin screw. Normal speed 20 knots.
PAINTWORK:	Hull black with white band, red boot-topping, white upper works, funnels red, white band and blue tops.
ORIGINAL PASS. ACCOM.:	500 1st, 377 cabin, 614 3rd, 1,432 steerage.

Described as one of the most magnificent cabin liners afloat, the lounge with its illuminated domed ceiling is a feature. Built for and owned by North German Lloyd Co. Was the largest ship owned by the Company before the war.

1914. Interned in New York.

1917. Seized by U.S. Government and used as troopship.

1919. U.S. Shipping Board.

1920. Sold to United States Mail Line. Converted to cabin class, later to United States Lines.

1932. Withdrawn from service and in September was towed to Chesapeake Bay by 7 tugs and laid up, too costly to run.

1935. It was suggested to the U.S. Government that she should be used as a training depot ship for training Merchant Marine seamen.

GEORGE WASHINGTON

No. 33. ATHLONE CASTLE. 1936

OWNERS:	The Union Castle Mail Steamship Co., Ltd.
SERVICE:	Southampton–Capetown via Madeira.
NAT. & PORT:	British. London.
BUILDERS:	Messrs. Harland & Wolff, Ltd., Belfast, 1936.
TONNAGE:	25,564 tons gross.
DIMENSIONS:	725 ft. lg. o.a., 680 ft. b.p. x 82 ft. beam. x 48 ft. depth. 6 decks.
ENGINES:	2 Harland-B & W. d.a. two cyls. 10 cyl. oil engines. cyl. diam. 66 m.m., c 1,500 mm. stroke, 24,000 b.h.p. Twin screw. Norma speed 19 knots.
EL. LT. & PWR.:	5 Diesel engine driven generators, each of 750 k.w. accommodate in a separate engine compartment.
PAINTWORK:	Hull Union-Castle grey, boot-topping red, upper works white, funne red with black top.
COMPLEMENT:	300 1st class passengers and 500 cabin class passengers.

Insulated cargo space of over 330,000 cubic feet for the carriage of fruits, etc and space for general cargo of 5,000 tons.

A sister ship and replica of the *Stirling Castle* except as to decorations an minor details, a third ship of the same type is being built, and to maintain th 14 day schedule set up by the *Stirling Castle* five of the older ships are to be re engined and modernised. First commander, Captain A. Barron. A specia feature of the tasteful and restful decorations is the splendid lighting system which throughout the public rooms is indirect. This splendid ship fully main tains and adds to the great traditions of the Line. The cabin class is speciall noticeable for its comfort and beautiful furnishings.

1935, Nov. 28th. Launched by H.R.H. the Princess Alice, Countess c Athlone.

1936, May 15th. She arrived at Southampton from the builders with 25 guests of the company on board. During the trip she was in close proximit with the *Queen Mary* and the commanders of the two great vessels exchange greetings.

1936, May 22nd. Left Southampton on her maiden voyage. She replace the fine old *Kenilworth Castle* of 1904.

ATHLONE CASTLE

[By courtesy of the Union Castle Line.

No. 34. STIRLING CASTLE. 1935

OWNERS:	The Union Castle Mail Steamship Co., Ltd.
SERVICE:	Southampton–Capetown via Madeira.
NAT. & PORT:	British. London.
BUILDERS:	Harland & Wolff, Ltd., Belfast, 1935.
TONNAGE:	25,550 tons gross.
DIMENSIONS:	725 ft. lg. o.a., 680 ft. lg. b.p. x 82 ft. beam. x 48 ft. depth. 6 decks.
ENGINES:	2 Harland-B & W. d.a. two cycle, 10 cyl. oil engines. Cyl diam. 660 mm. x 1,500 mm. stroke, 24,000 b.h.p. Twin screw. Normal speed 19 knots.
EL. LT. & PWR.:	5 Diesel engine driven generators, each of 750 k.w. accommodated in a separate engine compartment.
PAINTWORK:	Hull Union-Castle grey, boot-topping red, upper works white, funnel red with black top.
COMPLEMENT:	300 1st class and 500 cabin class passengers.

Insulated cargo space of 330,000 cubic feet for the carriage of fruits, etc., with certain compartments specially arranged for chilled and frozen produce. The characteristically high standard of the Line has been maintained in the ship's construction, the modern lines of the vessel with her curved rounded stem and cruiser stern giving the impression of speed and grace, whilst two masts and the single low streamlined funnel provide the finishing touch to a magnificent ship. There is ample deck space, the promenade deck and boat deck both being very extensive. The hull has eleven watertight bulkheads. The public rooms, consisting of dining room, smoking room, lounge, card room, drawing room, and verandah, are decorated in the modern style, comfort, convenience and artistic taste. The long gallery contains a well stocked library. The beautiful tiled swimming pool and well equipped gymnasium will cater for the sporting passengers, an electric elevator connects the swimming pool with the boat deck where sun bathing may be indulged in. The cabin class has also a complete set of very fine public rooms carried out with the same good taste in decorative work as the 1st class rooms. Hot and cold water is available in all staterooms in both classes and ventilating and heating by electricity is on a very efficient scale.

The two sisters were the largest ships launched in 1935, and with her sister ship they are the highest powered British motor ships.

1935, Aug. 18th. Launched, ceremony performed by Mrs. Robertson Gibbs, wife of the chairman of the Union Castle Mail S.S. Company.

1936, Feb. 7th. Maiden voyage commenced from Southampton.

1936, Aug. 24th. Left Southampton and inaugurated new voyage time taking only 14 days 1 hour instead of the usual 16 days and over. She easily accomplished this, beating the record held by the *Scot* for 43 years, her time being 14 days 18 hrs. 57 mins. Commander Stuart sent a telegram to Sir Edgar Britten before leaving Southampton congratulating the *Queen Mary* on her performance.

STIRLING CASTLE

[By permission of " Syren and Shipping"]

No. 35. LAFAYETTE. 1929

OWNERS:	Compagnie General Transatlantique, the French Line.
SERVICE:	Havre–New York and Cruising.
NAT. & PORT:	French. Havre.
BUILDERS:	Ch. & Atel. de St. Nazaire, St. Nazaire, France, 1929.
TONNAGE:	25,178 tons gross.
DIMENSIONS:	577·5 ft. lg. o.a. x 77 ft. 6 in. beam x 50 ft. depth. 5 decks.
ENGINES:	4 M.A.N. 6 cyl. d.a. 2 st. oil engines 18,000 b.h.p., cyl. dia. 23 in. x 35 in. st. (at 150 r.p.m.). Quad. screw. Normal speed 17 knots.
PAINTWORK:	Hull black with red boot-topping, funnel red with black top.
PASS. ACCOM.	591 cabin, 334 tourist, and 142 3rd class. Officers and crew, 472.

Sister ship to s.s. *Champlain* except as to engines.

Third ship of her name in French Line's fleet. Named after the famous Marquis de Lafayette whose aid to the American Colonists during the American revolution brought about the birth of a great nation. She is the first French trans-atlantic motor liner.

The hall forming the hub of social life on board is bright and gay; leading from it is the Grand Salon, sumptuous yet charmingly cosy, round the walls are portrayed episodes from the life of *Lafayette*, a richly old gold dome surmounts a group of rosewood columns. The dining saloon with tables for 2 and 4 persons has seats for 450 diners, with that touch and atmosphere of the famous restaurants of Paris. A roomy and comfortable library, with well stocked bookshelves, is a room of quiet and rest. The afternoon room with great bay windows, furnished in colourful harmony is an alluring spot for tea, a polished marquetry dance floor adds to its delights. The smoking room with a well equipped bar and restful furniture is a room of contentment. The café terrace with great windows on three sides giving an uninterrupted view of the ever changing ocean. The tourist accommodation is also excellent. Her unusual funnel and single mast are a noticeable feature.

1931-2. Came to London (Tilbury Landing Stage) on Cruise.

1934, Mar. Met terrible gale in Atlantic, hove to for five hours, upper works and 50 windows damaged.

LAFAYETTE

[By courtesy of the French Line

No. 36. EMPRESS OF SCOTLAND. 1905
(Ex Kaiserin Auguste Victoria.)

OWNERS:	Canadian Pacific Rly. Co.
SERVICE:	Southampton–Quebec.
NAT. & PORT:	British. London.
BUILDERS:	Akt. Ges. Vulkan, Stettin, Germany, 1905.
TONNAGE:	25,160 tons gross.
DIMENSIONS:	678 ft. lg. o.a. x 77·3 ft. beam x 50 ft. depth. 5 decks.
ENGINES:	2 Quad. exp. 4 cyl. engines. 18,000 s.h.p. Twin screw. Normal speed 17½ knots.
PAINTWORK:	Hull white with green boot-topping and blue band, funnels buff.

A very fine example of the pre-war Atlantic liner; although not built as a record maker, she was a very popular and luxurious vessel.

1905. Built (to be named *Europa*) for Hamburg-Amerika Line. Launched in presence of the German Emperor and Empress, and named in honour of the Empress.

1919. Ceded to Great Britain by Peace Treaty. Run by Shipping Controller and managed by Cunard Line.

1921. Sold to Canadian Pacific Railway. Refitted at Liverpool and renamed. Accommodation for 459 1st, 478 2nd, and 536 3rd class passengers. Became very popular both on Atlantic and for cruising.

1934. Sold to shipbreakers.

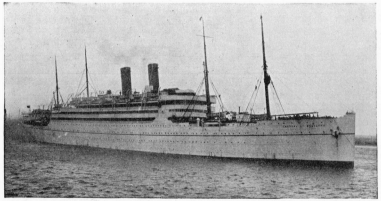

EMPRESS OF SCOTLAND

[*By courtesy of C.P.R. Co.*]

No. 37. ADRIATIC. 1906

OWNERS:	Cunard White Star Line.
SERVICE:	Liverpool–New York.
NAT. & PORT:	British. Liverpool.
BUILDERS:	Messrs. Harland & Wolff, Ltd., Belfast, 1906.
TONNAGE:	24,679 tons gross.
DIMENSIONS:	709 ft. lg. x 75·5 ft. beam x 52 ft. depth. 5 decks.
ENGINES:	2 Quad. exp. recip. engines, 4 cyl. 17,000 s.h.p. Twin screw. Normal speed 18 knots.
PAINTWORK:	Black hull with gold band, white upper works, funnels buff with black tops.
COMPLEMENT:	1,670 passengers. 557 officers and crew.

Largest ship of White Star Line's famous Big Four, and the largest ship in world to date. Known during the War as "Queen of the Munition Fleet" owing to her regular service on the New York–Liverpool run.

1922. When an electrician was fixing lights in a coal bunker, an explosion occurred, blowing off the hatches of No. 1 hold, sending a huge column of flames into the air. Five men were killed and three seriously injured. Captain H. F. David who was in command displayed great calmness and efficiency and under his able directions the outbreak was quickly got under control.

1933, Aug. 31st. Laid up at Liverpool.

1933, Oct. Chartered to take a large party of Boy Scouts for Mediterranean Cruise from March 19th to April 15th, 1934.

1934, Dec. Sold to Japanese shipbreakers for £62,000.

[By courtesy of Cunard White Star Line

ADRIATIC

No. 38. CONTE BIANCAMANO. 1925

OWNERS:	Italia Line.
SERVICE:	Genoa–New York.
NAT. & PORT:	Italian. Genoa.
BUILDERS:	Sir Wm. Beardmore & Co., Ltd., Glasgow, 1925.
TONNAGE:	24,416 tons gross.
DIMENSIONS:	650 ft. lg. x 76 ft. beam. x 27 ft. depth. 4 decks.
ENGINES:	4 steam turbines d.r. geared. 24,000 s.h.p. Twin screws. Normal speed 20 knots.
BOILERS:	7 D.E. & 2 S.E. boilers, stm. pr. 220 lbs. F.D.
PAINTWORK:	Black hull, red boot-topping with white dividing line, white upper works, funnels white with green band and red tops.

Sister ship to *Conte Grande* but slightly smaller. Very fine medium sized liner with perfect artistic taste in decorations and furnishings. Public rooms consisting of vestibule, ballroom, entrance hall, dining saloon, library, writing room, children's room, verandah café, gymnasium and swimming pool and all the refinements to be found on the large express liners. She has wide open deck space for promenading and deck games.

This ship was built and run at first in the Fleet of Lloyd Sabaudo Company, during which time she sailed under their colours, the funnel at that time being yellow with white bands between two blue bands. Later Lloyd Sabaudo Company merged into the Italia Line.

1933, Oct. An unusual charge against a liner was brought in New York by a man named David Warshauer, who claimed £40,000 from her owners that the vessel refused to stop to pick him up, when he was carried out to sea in his motor boat, in a gale. He and his companion were adrift for eight days and on the sixth day he claims that the liner came so close to them that he could see passengers leaning over the rails and could hear the orchestra playing. His companion died and he was lamed as a result of exposure. The ship's officers deny seeing the motor boat or the distress signals. Nothing further appeared about this extraordinary charge.

1935. Employed as troopship to East Africa.

CONTE BIANCAMANO

[By courtesy of "Italia" Line

No. 39. WASHINGTON. 1932

OWNERS:	The United States Lines.
SERVICE:	New York–Plymouth and Hamburg.
NAT. & PORT:	United States. New York.
BUILDERS:	The New York Shipbuilding Corporation, Camden, N.J., U.S.A., 1932.
TONNAGE:	24,299 tons gross.
DIMENSIONS:	705 ft. lg. o.a. x 86 ft. beam x 47 ft. depth. 8 passenger decks.
ENGINES:	6 steam turbines. 30,000 s.h.p. Twin screw. Normal speed 20 knots.
BOILERS:	6 Babcock & Wilcox water tube, 400 lbs. 670 deg. s.h. F.D. Oil fuel.
COMPLEMENT:	500 cabin, 500 tourist, and 200 3rd class.
PAINTWORK:	Hull black, upper works white, funnels red with white band and blue tops.

With sister ship *Manhattan* they are the two largest liners as yet built in the U.S.A. Most luxurious cabin class liners. One great deck is devoted to the public rooms consisting of Palm Court, two galleries, Grand Salon, writing room, library, smoking lounge, verandah café; these magnificent rooms with the glass enclosed promenades cover the whole of the promenade deck. The tourist class is well catered for with spacious lounge, smoking room, foyer, children's room, and beautiful dining room. The third class accommodation is exceptionally good, having dining saloon, smoking room and lounge, every stateroom having hot and cold running water and wardrobes and an electric oscillating fan, and a dressing table. A complete air conditioning plant is installed which regulates not only temperature but humidity. A sister ship to replace the *Leviathan* is to be built.

WASHINGTON

No. 40. MANHATTAN. 1931

OWNERS:	The United States Lines.
SERVICE:	New York–Plymouth and Hamburg.
NAT. & PORT:	United States. New York.
BUILDERS:	The New York Shipbuilding Corporation, Camden, N.J., U.S.A., 1931.
TONNAGE:	24,289 tons gross.
DIMENSIONS:	705 ft. lg. o.a. x 86 ft. beam x 47 ft. depth. 8 passenger decks.
ENGINES:	6 steam turbines s.r. geared. 30,000 s.h.p. Twin screw. Normal speed 20 knots.
BOILERS:	6 Babcock & Wilcox express boilers, water tube, stm. pr. 400 lbs. sq. in. 682 deg. S.H. F.D. Oil fuel.
EL. LT. & PWR.:	4 Westinghouse steam turbo-generators 500 k.w.
PAINTWORK:	Hull black, red boot-topping with white dividing line, white upper works, funnels red with white band and blue tops.
COMPLEMENT:	500 cabin, 500 tourist, 200 3rd class passengers.
REMARKS:	Cargo capacity is 380,000 cubic feet.

Like her sister ship her hull is divided into twelve watertight compartments. There are steel hatchway covers, and all lifeboats are built of copper bearing steel to resist corrosion, twenty-four in all. Air conditioning plant for dining saloons, Punkah-Louve ventilation for all staterooms together with a 12 in. oscillating electric fan. Most cabin class rooms have private baths and there are twelve suites-de-luxe, an innovation in a cabin class liner. The whole of the promenade deck between the glass enclosed promenades is taken up with the large and beautiful public rooms. An impressive ship both as to external appearance and internally. The cabin smoking room is in the American Indian style with wood burning open fire place. The Palm Court is in Chinese Chippendale. The lounge has a stage for entertainments, "Talkie" apparatus and a dance floor. A swimming pool and gymnasium are also provided.

1930, Dec. 8th. Keel laid.

1931, Dec. 5th. Launched.

1932, Aug. 10th. Maiden voyage commenced from New York.

1934, Mar. Was hove-to for 18 hours in tremendous Atlantic gale.

MANHATTAN

[By courtesy of U.S. Lines

No. 41. ROTTERDAM. 1908

OWNERS:	Holland-Amerika Line.
SERVICE:	Rotterdam–New York.
NAT. & PORT:	Dutch. Rotterdam.
BUILDERS:	Messrs. Harland & Wolff, Ltd., Belfast, 1908.
TONNAGE:	24,149 tons gross.
DIMENSIONS:	650 ft. lg. o.a. x 77 ft. beam x 44 ft. depth. Draught 33 ft. 4 decks.
ENGINES:	2 Quad. exp. recip. engines. 4 cyl. 14,500 s.h.p. Twin screw. Normal speed 17 knots.
BOILERS:	8 D.E. and S.E. boilers, stm. pr. 215 lbs.
PAINTWORK:	Hull black, red boot-topping, upper works white, funnels buff with one white band between two green.

Rotterdam was the name of the first steamer of the line in 1855, she was 1,700 tons. The second *Rotterdam* was the ex-*British Empire* bought in 1886. A third was built in 1895. The largest pre-war Dutch liner. A comfortable if somewhat slow speed liner, very popular both on her regular service and on cruising. The Line established in 1855 maintains a regular Rotterdam–New York service as well as other minor services. Owing to large War losses by the Line she was laid up at Rotterdam for greater part of the War.

1935, Sept. 30th. When returning from a West Indian cruise to New York with 424 passengers and crew of 500 she was driven ashore in gale which raged all over the West Indies and Central America. Her commander, Capt. Van Dulken, wirelessed that ship was in no immediate danger, but in need of assistance, the seas having gone down. Next day the passengers were taken off by a British steamship.

1935, Nov. 2nd. After repairs she left New York for Rotterdam.

ROTTERDAM

No. 42. STRATHMORE. 1935

OWNERS:	The Peninsular & Oriental Steam Navigation Co.
SERVICE:	London–India–Australia.
NAT. & PORT:	British. London.
BUILDERS:	Messrs. Vickers, Armstrong Co., Ltd., Barrow, 1935.
TONNAGE:	24,000 tons gross.
DIMENSIONS:	665 ft. lg. o.a., 630 ft. lg. b.p. x 82 ft. beam. 8 decks.
ENGINES:	2 sets of Parsons steam turbines, each set comprising 1 h.p. 1 Med pr. and 1 l.p. turbine, driving separate pinions engaging the main gear wheel. 24,000 s.h.p. Twin screw. Normal speed 24 knots.
BOILERS:	6 Babcock & Wilcox water tube boilers, stm. pr. 440 lbs. super heated to 725 deg. F. Arranged to burn oil fuel only.
EL. LT. & PWR.:	Brown Bros. 4 cyl. Electro-hydraulic steering gear with duplicate power units. Grimmel fire sprinkler system fitted throughout vessel 3 Turbo-electric generating sets by the B.T.H. Co., Ltd., each 550 kilowatts at 230 volts.
PAINTWORK:	Hull and upper works white, boot-topping red and funnel buff.
COMPLEMENT:	445 1st, 665 tourist class. Officers and crew, 510.
REMARKS:	Space for 8,000 tons of cargo.

Sports and games area on "A" deck 275 ft. long by 82 ft. wide. Ship's "Lido" consists of bathing pool, verandah café, and Cocktail bar. She possesses all the refinements of sea travel so much appreciated in her two immediate predecessors. Largest ship as yet built for the P. & O. Line and the largest ship on Indian and Australian trade. Every device and amenity for the comfort and safety of passengers has been provided. Her design and external appearance closely resembles the *Orion*, except that she has two masts and different colouring Capt. F. Sudell first commander.

1935, April 4th. Launched by H.R.H. the Duchess of York, launching weight 13,000 tons.

1935, Sept. 11th. Left Barrow for Birkenhead for dry docking before steam trials.

1935, Sept. 15th. Steam trials on Firth of Clyde, in most unfavourable wind did a mean speed of just under 22 knots in two directions, her highest speed being 22·27 knots.

1935, Sept. 20th. The Company gave a dinner on board to 400 guests.

1935, Sept. 27th. Maiden voyage, a cruise to Madeira and Canary Islands etc.

1935, Oct.–Nov. On her first voyage to India she beat the record held by the Italian *Victoria* by steaming from Marseilles to Bombay in exactly 10 days The Italian ship's record is from Genoa to Bombay in 11 days, a distance 102 miles less. *Strathmore* is reported to have done an average of 20·07 knots, and after clearing Suez Canal an average of 20·56 knots.

1936, Jan. Captain Sudell, her popular commander, retired and was super seded by Captain Harrison of the *Strathnaver*.

1936, Jan. The P. & O. Company announce that they have ordered two more similar ships from the same builders.

STRATHMORE

[By courtesy of P. & O. Line

No. 43. VULCANIA. 1928

OWNERS:	Italia Line. (Cosulich Soc. Triestino di Navigatione.)
SERVICE:	Trieste–New York.
NAT. & PORT:	Italian. Trieste.
BUILDERS:	Cantiera Nav. Triestino, Monfalcone, Italy, 1928.
TONNAGE:	23,970 tons gross.
DIMENSIONS:	651 ft. 10 in. o.a., lg., 631·4 ft. lg. b.p. x 79·8 ft. beam x 24·4 ft. depth. 6 pass. decks.
ENGINES:	2 8 cyl. 4 st. d.a. B. & W. oil motors. Cyl. 33 1/16 in. dia. by 59 in. stroke. 24,000 B.H.P. Twin screw. Normal speed 19½ knots.
PAINTWORK:	Hull black, upper works white, funnel white, green band, red top.
ORIG. PAINTWK.:	Hull black, upper works white, funnel red with white band and narrow black top.

The *Vulcania* and her sister ship *Saturnia* are a fine pair of motor cabin class liners, very roomy and comfortable, their decorations and furnishings leave nothing to be desired and the tourist class is notable for its excellent accommodation, the former second class having been added to the tourist class. They are very popular with American travellers who wish to take the Mediterranean route to Europe.

1935. New Fiat engines fitted 26,000 s.h.p. to give speed of 21 knots.

1935, Dec. After being re-fitted with new engines, which are claimed to be the most powerful heavy oil engines ever fitted in a ship, on trials she made a speed of 23·33 knots. She resumed service from Trieste to New York on December 21st.

1936, Oct. 19th. On voyage from Naples to New York fire broke out on board in the 3rd class section which was unoccupied. Several tugs and liners went to her assistance but the outbreak was put out by the ship's company and her own apparatus, and she proceeded on her voyage.

VULCANIA
(Under original colours)

[By courtesy of Cosulich Line]

No. 44. SATURNIA. 1927

OWNERS:	Italia Line. (Cosulich Soc. Triestina di Navigatione.)
SERVICE:	Trieste–New York.
NAT. & PORT:	Italian. Trieste.
BUILDERS:	Cantiere Navale Triestino, Monfalcone, Italy, 1927.
TONNAGE:	23,940 tons gross.
DIMENSIONS:	651 ft. lg. o.a., 631 ft. lg. b.p. x 80 ft. beam x 24·4 ft. depth. 6 decks
ENGINES:	2 8 cyl. 4 st. d.a. B. & W. oil motors. 24,000 s.h.p. Twin screw Normal speed 19½ knots.
PAINTWORK:	Hull black with white upper works, funnel white with red top and green band.

Sister ship *Vulcania*. In external appearance and appointments these two fine motor vessels are alike. Both have excellent cabin and tourist class accommodation.

1935. Fitted with new Sulzer engines to give speed of 21 knots, 26,000 s.h.p.

1935, Aug. 24th. Trooping with Italian troops to East Africa.

SATURNIA

[By courtesy of "Italia" Line

No. 45. BALTIC. 1904

OWNERS:	The White Star Line.
SERVICE:	Liverpool–New York.
NAT. & PORT:	British. Liverpool.
BUILDERS:	Messrs. Harland & Wolff, Ltd., Belfast, 1904.
TONNAGE:	23,876 tons gross.
DIMENSIONS:	709 ft. long x 75·6 ft. beam x 52 ft. 6 in. depth. 5 decks.
ENGINES:	2 Quad. exp. 4 cyl. steam engines. 15,000 s.h.p. Twin screw. Normal speed 17 knots.
PAINTWORK:	Hull black, with gold band, boot-topping red, upper works white, funnels buff with black tops.
COMPLEMENT:	1,428 passengers, 542 officers and crew.

Largest ship launched to date. Second ship of the name, the first was one of the original four steamers of Line in 1871. She was the third of the famous White Star "Big Four," and for some inexplicable reason was the most popular.

1909, Jan. 23rd. Received S O S from sinking *Republic*. Took off the passengers who had been taken on board *Florida* which had collided with *Republic* and took them to New York, the *Republic* sinking shortly afterwards. One of the very earliest rescues made by wireless.

1911, April 14th. Received S O S from sinking *Titanic* and steamed towards her for 9 hours and then heard from *Carpathia* that *Titanic* had sunk.

1914-8. Carried over 32,000 Canadian and American troops to France.

1917, April. Was unsuccessfully attacked by submarines on two days running.

1933, Jan. Sold to Japanese shipbreakers for £33,000 along with the *Megantic* of the same Line.

BALTIC

No. 46. FRANCE. 1912

OWNERS:	Compagnie Generale Transatlantique, the French Line.
SERVICE:	Havre–New York.
NAT. & PORT:	French. Havre.
BUILDERS:	Ch. & Atel. de St. Nazaire, St. Nazaire, France, 1912.
TONNAGE:	23,769 tons gross.
DIMENSIONS:	690 ft. lg. x 76 ft. beam x 49 ft. depth. 5 decks.
ENGINES:	4 steam turbines (Parsons). 42,000 s.h.p. Quad. screw. Normal speed 24 knots.
BOILERS:	11 D.E. & 8 S.E. Coal consumption 720 tons per day.
PAINTWORK:	Black hull, white upper works with red boot-topping. Funnels red with black top.
COMPLEMENT:	Passengers: 535 1st, 442 2nd, 948 3rd class. Officers and crew 600.

First French Turbine liner. Very luxurious for her day.

1909, Feb. Laid down.

1910, Sept. 20th. Launched. Largest French liner to date.

1912, April. Speed trials did 25 knots, making her next fastest liner to *Lusitania* and *Mauretania*. Was delayed on trials by fire in her coal bunkers.

1912, Aug. 20th. Maiden voyage, Havre to New York. Held up on her second voyage by lightning strike of her crew. Was sent to Southampton after a few voyages, where Messrs. Harland & Wolff, Ltd., extended her bilge keels and changed two of her propellers. On her next voyage she broke her own record by returning from New York to Havre in 5 days 17 hours.

1914, Aug. Commissioned in French Navy as *France IV*, and later went to Dardanelles as armed transport, later serving as Hospital ship, and in 1917-8 was transporting American troops.

1919. Had explosion on board killing nine men.

1919, Aug. Returned to normal service.

1924. Thoroughly overhauled, converted to oil burning, and passenger accommodation reconstructed by builders.

1928. On cruising service.

1932, Sept. Laid up at Havre.

1933, Jan. 7th. Fire on board in dock at Havre, only watchmen on board.

1934, Nov. Sold to Dunkirk shipbreakers for scrapping.

1935, Nov. Caught fire whilst being dismantled.

FRANCE

By courtesy of the French Line

No. 47. ORION. 1935

OWNERS:	The Orient Line.
SERVICE:	London–Ceylon–Australian ports, and cruising.
NAT. & PORT:	British. Barrow.
BUILDERS:	Messrs. Vickers Armstrong, Ltd., Barrow-in-Furness, 1935.
TONNAGE:	23,371 tons gross.
DIMENSIONS:	665 ft. lg. o.a., 630 ft. lg. b.p. x 84 ft. beam x 47 ft. 6 in. depth to E deck. Draught 30 ft. 8 passenger decks.
ENGINES:	2 sets of Parsons steam turbines, with sin. red. gearing, 1,175/112 r.p.m. 24,000 s.h.p. Twin screw. Normal speed 21 knots.
BOILERS:	6 Babcock & Wilcox water tube, 4 large and 2 smaller, fitted with super-heaters and tubular air heaters. Stm. pr. 450 lbs., 750 deg. s.h. Oil fuel. Forced draught.
EL. LT. & PWR.:	3 main turbo-generators, each 500 k.w. at 220 volts. and 1 auxiliary Diesel engine-generator 90 k.w. 220 volt. Grimmel fire sprinkler system fitted throughout. An air conditioning plant is installed not only to regulate temperature but humidity of the incoming air as well; first plant of its kind installed in a British liner.
PAINTWORK:	Hull corn coloured with green boot-topping, white upper works, funnel buff.
COMPLEMENT:	486 1st, 653 tourist class passengers, 466 officers and crew.

She has a very spacious games deck, longer than four cricket pitches and wider than Piccadilly at the Ritz Hotel including side walks. Cargo hatchways are flush with decks, and a new feature is that the lifeboats are mounted on patent davits above the deck to give valuable space and a clear outlook to sea. The dignity of the public rooms is attained by a new way in the decorative scheme, no elaborate carvings, and yet magnificence, from restrained colouring. The lounge is a work of art in cheery mahogany of a cool pink grain, the library has the unusual feature of a pair of folding doors which protect the altar used for Sunday Chapel. The after gallery and dancing space is not only divided by a wonderful glass wall, but same is removable; farther aft is the café, here an effect of considerable brilliance is achieved, the furniture is leather-covered in grey-green, with white piping; chief among the sights from the café verandah is the swimming pool and lido. The pool is of blue tiles, with constantly running sea water. Near the pool is the Tavern containing a bar. The saloon dining room is panelled with cool weathered sycamore and lighter burr wood, the curtains are of cream colour with a design in two blues to pick up the blue leather upholstery of the chairs, a shallow dome surmounts the central portion and there are two walls of mirror. Said to have cost over £1,000,000.

1934, Dec. Launched by wireless by H.R.H. the Duke of Gloucester from Brisbane, Queensland, the first British ship to be so launched.

1935, July 31st. On speed trials did 21·6 knots.

1935, Aug. 15th. Maiden voyage, Mediterranean cruise. On Sept. 5th when homeward bound she received S O S from *Doric* and took off 500 passengers. It was announced in October that a sister ship had been ordered.

ORION

No. 48. DUILIO. 1923

OWNERS:	Italia Line.
SERVICE:	Genoa–South Africa.
NAT. & PORT:	Italian. Genoa.
BUILDERS:	G. Ansaldo & Co., Sestri, Ponent, Italy, 1923.
TONNAGE:	23,635 tons gross.
DIMENSIONS:	635 ft. 6 in. lg. o.a., 601·4 ft. lg. b.p. x 75·9 ft. beam x 50 ft. depth. 6 pass. decks.
ENGINES:	2 sets of steam turbines. 22,000 s.h.p. Twin screw. Normal speed 21 knots.
BOILERS:	6 D.E. & 4 S.E. boilers. 200 lbs. stm. pr. Oil fuel.
PAINTWORK:	White hull with green band and green boot-topping. Funnels white with green band and red tops.

With her sister ship *Giulio Cesare* they are an elegant pair of steamships carrying 1st, 2nd and tourist class passengers. A great vestibule, lounge, ballroom, dining saloon, club on boat deck, open air swimming pool with its lido and gymnasium adjoining, are provided for the 1st class.

1933, Sept. 21st. Arrived at Genoa for extensive overhaul for service on the Mediterranean–Cape service in competition with Union-Castle Line.

DUILIO   *[By courtesy of " Italia " Lin*

No. 49. QUEEN OF BERMUDA. 1933

OWNERS:	Furness Withy & Co., Ltd.
SERVICE:	New York–Bermudas, and Cruising.
NAT. & PORT:	British. London.
BUILDERS:	Vickers Armstrong, Ltd., Barrow-in-Furness, 1933.
TONNAGE:	22,575 gross register tons.
DIMENSIONS:	579·5 ft. length o.a., 550 ft. lg. b.p. x 83·5 ft. ex. brdth. x 42 ft. depth. Draught 26 ft. 3 in. 6 passenger decks.
ENGINES:	2 steam turbine-generators, each 7,500 k.w., 10,000 h.p. 3,000 r.p.m. 3,000 volts. 4 synchronous electric motors on screw shafts totalling 19,300 s.h.p. 150 r.p.m. By the General Electric Co., Ltd., of London and Witton. 4 screws. Normal speed 20 knots.
BOILERS:	8 Babcock & Wilcox water tube, 400 lbs. stm. pr., 675 deg. s.h. Oil fuel. Forced draught.
EL. LT. & PWR.:	4 General Electric turbo-generators 750 k.w. each.
PAINTWORK:	Grey hull, green boot-topping with white dividing line, white upper works, funnels black with one broad and one narrow red band.
COMPLEMENT:	731 1st class passengers, 40 of which may be accommodated as second class.
REMARKS:	12 lifeboats for 99 persons each and 2 emergency boats each for 55 persons, all fitted with Fleming's hand propelling gear.

In addition to the main generators and motors there are 270 electric motors on board fitted to pumps, fans and other auxiliaries; eleven "Express" lifts, electric cooking equipment, 600 cabin fans, 430 line telephone installation, and 20,000 lamps and lighting fittings all supplied by the G. E. Co., Ltd. With her sister ship *Monarch of Bermuda* these fine electric ships are known as the "Millionaires' ships." They are the largest and most luxurious vessels ever to be built for such a short run, of under 700 miles; they make a round trip in 84 hours, allowing 12 hours in port; this both ships have carried out practically continuously which speaks well for the fast manoeuvring qualities and reliability of electrical propelled vessels. It is said that they are the only liners afloat with private bath to every stateroom. The public rooms are exceptionally beautiful and spacious, the dining room treated in sycamore and walnut with some colour lacquer work, has a faint "Chinese" style in some of its decorative details. Immediately forward of the dining room is the "Foyer" with the "Nubian" cocktail bar leading off. The library is named "Homer" and is an exquisite room panelled with a new veneer named "Bubinga." Two writing rooms, one on each side of the ship, lead from the library. Aft of the library is situated the "Forum" lounge, a truly magnificent room fitted with complete stage for theatrical and "Talkie" entertainments; the colour scheme is pleasant mellow gold; the height of the lounge ceiling is 22 ft. Amidships is the palatial entrance hall leading aft to the "Osiris" verandah café and a further café named "Isis." The great dance hall is named most appropriately "Elysium," adjoining which is another beautifully modern cocktail bar. The smoke room is one of the most beautiful rooms afloat, panelled in grey-brown English oak with a raised ceiling 18 ft. high. The Silver Lagoon swimming bath hall is one of the most perfectly beautiful swimming pools ever constructed. There is also a gymnasium, shops, beauty salons, etc. This splendid ship was built in 14 months to replace the *Bermuda* lost by fire when refitting at Belfast in November, 1931.

1932, Jan.   Laid down.

1932, Sept. 1st.   Launched.

1933, Feb. 13th.   Steam trials, she touched a speed of 21 knots, with an average of 20·7.

1933, April.   Left Liverpool on her maiden voyage to New York.

1933, May 7th.   Left New York on her first voyage to Bermuda.

1933.   She made a record run from Sandy Hook, N.Y., to St. David's Head in 32 hrs. 48 mins. at an average speed of 20·33 knots, beating the previous record held by the *Monarch of Bermuda* by half a knot.   Since going into commission she has almost regularly been in and out of port every fifty or so hours. During the year she steams some 100,000 miles, making 150 arrivals and departures, records that have probably never been surpassed by any ocean-going vessels.

QUEEN OF BERMUDA

By courtesy of Furness Withy & Co. Ltd.

No. 50. AMERICA. 1905
(ex Amerika)

OWNERS: United States Lines.
SERVICE: New York–Europe.
NAT. & PORT: United States. New York.
BUILDERS: Messrs. Harland & Wolff, Ltd., Belfast, 1905.
TONNAGE: 22,622 tons gross.
DIMENSIONS: 668·8 ft. lg. o.a., 74·3 ft. beam x 47 ft. depth. 5 decks.
ENGINES: 2 Quad. exp. 4 cyl. engines. 11,000 s.h.p. Twin screw. Normal
               speed 17½ knots.
PAINTWORK: Black hull, red boot-topping with white dividing line, white upper
               works, funnel red with white band and blue tops.

Ex Hamburg-Amerika Line. Built for big emigration trade, but also has excellent saloon and cabin accommodation which was converted by the U.S. Lines into cabin, tourist and 3rd class. A fine example of pre-war liner of a type that is fast disappearing, with her straight stem, counter stern, four masts and two tall narrow funnels. She was the first Atlantic liner to have restaurant where meals were served *À La Carte.*

1909, Jan. Rescued crew of sinking Italian steamer *Florida* which sunk after collision with *Republic.*

1907, April. Ran aground in River Elbe.

1907. Aground off Altonburgh.

1910. Had £8,000 jewel robbery on board.

1911. Rammed British submarine off Kent coast; 15 lives lost.

1913. Aground off Staten Island, New York Bay, U.S.

1914, Aug. Remained in Boston Harbour after declaration of war and was interned.

1917. Seized by U.S. War Dept. While refitting at Hoboken pier, was sunk. Raised and refitted as troopship.

1923. Managed by U.S. Lines.

1926. Caught fire at Newport News. Damage to the extent of £400,000.

1932. Laid up as a reserve transport for the U.S. Navy.

AMERICA

No. 51. STRATHNAVER. 1931

Owners:	Peninsular & Oriental Steam Navigation Co.
Service:	London–India–Australia, and Cruising.
Nat. & Port:	British. London.
Builders:	Messrs. Vickers Armstrong, Ltd., Barrow, 1931.
Tonnage:	22,547 tons gross.
Dimensions:	664 ft. lg. o.a., 630 ft. lg.b.p. x 80·1 ft. beam x 46·5 ft. depth. Draugh 29 ft. 2 in. 9 decks.
Engines:	2 steam turbo-generators, 21,400 k.w. 3,000 V. 3,000 r.p.m. 2 electri motors, synchronous type. 125 r.p.m. 3 p.h. 3,000 volts. each 14,00 s.h.p., total 28,000 s.h.p., by The British Thomson-Houston Co. Ltd., Rugby. Twin screw. Normal speed 22 knots.
Boilers:	4 Yarrow water tube, oil fired boilers, stm. pr. 425 lbs., super heate to temp. of 725 deg. F., 2 auxiliary boilers, all arranged in 1 stokehold
El. Lt. & Pwr.:	3 B.T.H. turbo-generators ea. 750 k.w., 220 volts., 1 B.T.H. turbo generator 400 k.w. 220 volts for port duty.
Paintwork:	Hull white with red boot-topping, upper works white, funnels buff
Complement:	498 1st. class, 670 tourist class. Officers and crew 487.

Until advent of *Strathmore* and *Orion* in 1935 "the two white sisters," as the *Strathnaver* and *Strathaird* are called, were the two largest and fastest liners in Indian and Australian trades. Decorations and furniture being beautiful but restrained in the modern manner. Verandah lounge and two swimming pools are a special feature. Name taken from one of the titles of the late Earl of Inchcape, Chairman of the Company.

1930, Feb. Launched. On trials made 23·1 knots over the measured mile.

1931, Oct. 2nd. Maiden voyage from Tilbury.

1933, Jan. 13th. Met with severe southerly gale in channel and hove-to for four hours outside Plymouth, homeward bound from Australia with passengers, mails and specie.

1936, Sept. She returned from a Mediterranean Cruise, having maintained an average of 21.65 knots for 24 hrs., believed to be a P. & O. record.

STRATHNAVER

[By courtesy of P. & O. Line

No. 52. STRATHAIRD. 1932

OWNERS:	Peninsular & Oriental Steam Navigation Co.
SERVICE:	London–India–Australia, and Cruising.
NAT. & PORT:	British. London.
BUILDERS:	Messrs. Vickers Armstrong, Ltd., Barrow, 1932.
TONNAGE:	22,544 tons gross.
DIMENSIONS:	664 ft. lg. o.a., 630 ft. lg. b.p. x 80·2 ft. beam x 46 ft. depth. Draught 29 ft. 9 decks.
ENGINES:	2 steam turbo-generators, 21,400 k.w., 3,000 V., 3,000 r.p.m. 2 electric motors, synchronous type, 125 r.p.m., 3 ph., 3,000 volts. each, 14,000 s.h.p., total 28,000 s.h.p. By British Thomson-Houston Co., Ltd., Rugby. Twin screw. Normal speed 22 knots.
BOILERS:	4 Yarrow water tube, oil fired boilers, stm. pr. 425 lbs., super heated to temp. of 725 deg. F., 2 auxiliary boilers, all arranged in one stokehold.
EL. LT. & PWR.:	3 B.T.H. turbo-generators, ea. 750 k.w. 220 volts and 1 B.T.H. ditto for port duty 400 k.w., 220 volts.
PAINTING:	Hull white with red boot-topping, upper works white, funnels buff.
COMPLEMENT:	498 1st, 668 tourist class. Officers and crew, 487.

Until advent of *Strathmore* and *Orion* in 1935 she and her sister ship were the largest and fastest ships in the Indian and Australian trades. Six decks have open-air promenades, the public rooms are very luxuriously decorated and furnished in the modern style. Verandah lounge and two swimming pools and "Talkies" being provided, as well as a well-equipped gymnasium. All electric cooking. Very successful ships in service, and steam as quietly and vibrationlessly as a sailing ship.

1931, July 18th. Launched. On steam trials did 23·11 knots.

1932, Feb. 12th. Maiden voyage from Tilbury.